A Powerful Marriage

"Learning to Live Happily Ever-After"

By
David A. Farmer, PhD

TEACH Services, Inc.
Brushton, New York

PRINTED IN CANADA
World rights reserved. This book or any portion thereof may not be copied or reproduced in any form or manner whatever, except as provided by law, without the written permission of the publisher, except by a reviewer who may quote brief passages in a review.

2002 03 04 05 06 07 08 09 10 11 · 5 4 3 2 1

The author assumes full responsibility for the accuracy of all facts and quotations as cited in this book.

Copyright © 2002 TEACH Services, Inc.
ISBN 1-57258-225-1
Library of Congress Catalog Card No. 2002103224

Unless otherwise noted, Scripture quotations are taken from the HOLY BIBLE, KING JAMES VERSION.

Scripture taken from the HOLY BIBLE, NEW INTERNATIONAL VERSION.

Copyright 1973, 1978, 1984 International Bible Society—Used by permission.

Quotations taken from the writings of Ellen G. White are referenced by publication and page number.

The author assumes full responsibility for all facts, use of quotations, and references cited in this syllabus.

Published by

TEACH Services, Inc.
www.tsibooks.com

Table of Contents

Meet the Author iv
A Message from the author v
A Special Thanks: vi
Introduction vii
"Learning to Live Happily Ever After" 1
"What are Temperaments?" 8
"University of Hard Knocks" 12
"Lord Have Mercy, I Married a Motor-Mouth Joker:
    The Sanguine" 19
"Help! I Married an Egotistical and Domineering
    Workaholic: *The Choleric*" 29
"The Six Million-Dollar Man and the Bionic Woman:
    The Melancholy" 41
"The Tenacious Peacemaker:
    The Phlegmatic" 52
"There is Hope" 57
"Determinations" 68
"Mask or Not to Mask; That is the Question" 73
"Myths of a Happy or Miserable Marriage" 87
"The Y2Khaos of Marriage." 99
"God's Pillars for a Happy Marriage" 108
"Why Do Such Good Looking Ladies Marry Such
    Ugly Looking Men?" 117
"The Storms of Marriage" 132
"How to Survive and Revive a Dead Marriage" 147
"Strong to the Finish" 157
INDEX TO REFERENCES
Introduction 169

Meet the Author

David Farmer received his Ph.D. in Christian Counseling from Christian Bible College and Seminary in Independence, Missouri. He is currently working toward a Doctor of Ministry. In 1997 he was ordained into the ministry of the Seventh-day Adventist Church. He is the author of two books; *Power Witnessing – How to Reach Different Personalities for Christ* (Review and Herald Publishing Association, 1999) and *A Powerful Marriage – Learning to Live Happily Ever-After*.

He and his wife, Kathy, have three children, Tonya, David Jr., and Charles Newkirk. They have two dogs, Alpine and Tabby.

A Message from the author

Thank you for purchasing this book. This easy to read book is about learning the language your spouse and children speak and why they do what they do. Even if you have already read many books on temperaments, you'll find this volume takes a little different twist from the others.

I pray this manuscript will bring you closer to Christ and those around you as you *Learn to Live Happily Ever-After*.

David Farmer
February 2001

A Special Thanks:

I would like to give a salute to some very special people who made this book possible.

First to *James Hunt* and *Sharryn Mahorney* for all the time they took to cross my "t's" and dot my "i's." For their patience of correcting my Texas grammar and concealing my accent.

To my *church members* for their patience, endurance, calmness, and being merciful toward me while I worked on this publication.

To my *friends and family members* who allowed me to use some of their life stories, for many, I'm sure, were truly embarrassing to them.

And to *Tonya, David Jr., and Kirk*. The ones who were above all, the most patient and long-suffering for permitting me to expose their weak, as well as their strong, points of character.

And most of all, to my dear and loving wife Kathy the one who has brought me true happiness for over two decades. She has convinced me there truly can be found heavenly peace here on this earth.

Pastor David A. Farmer, Ph. D.,
davidfarmer@prodigy.net

Introduction

"If there is any subject which should be carefully considered and in which the counsel of older and more experienced persons should be sought, *it is the subject of marriage*; if ever the Bible was needed as a counselor, if ever divine guidance should be sought in prayer, it is before taking a step that binds persons together for life."[1] "It is often the case that persons before marriage have little opportunity to become acquainted with each other's *habits and disposition*, and, so far as everyday life is concerned, *they are virtually strangers when they unite their interests at the altar*."[2] "Everywhere are seen wrecks of humanity, broken-down family altars, ruined homes." [3]

Do you want a richer, fuller, and more enjoyable and rewarding marriage? That's probably like asking if you would object to winning the ten million-dollar sweepstakes from Dick Clark and Ed McMahon with the taxes prepaid. Of course you want, and in most cases need, a more rewarding and richer marriage with no strings attached. Even if you have a good marriage, it couldn't hurt to have one better. A great marriage has the power to keep our spirit happy unlike any other experience, just as an unhappy marriage has the power to dampen our spirit unlike any other.

How are you feeling about your marriage right now? When it comes to your day-to-day functions as a married spouse, how would you describe the directions of your thoughts and moods toward your partner in marriage? What is going on in the closet of your mind as you ponder yesterday's events of your marriage? Are you cherishing or hating them?

This book is designed to help individuals and couples to strengthen and enhance their marriage. Admittedly, a lot of books have the same goal. Today, there is a large number of books, instructional videos, and magazines teaching how to have a happier marriage. How is this book any different? In *A Powerful Marriage, Learning to Live Happily Ever-After*, I have gone beyond the distinct condensed advice so many of the others offer. I go farther than just proposing a prescription that offers instant problem solving. Throughout this entire volume you will find easy-to-relate-to anecdotes with many amusing life experiences. There are commentaries from people who have learned the easy and hard way of how to have a successful and happy marriage.

If you are married, have ever been married, or are thinking about getting married, then chances are you have had some ups and downs in your marriage or courtship. The chances are you have had more downs than ups. In some homes many days go by with never a word of encouragement or sign of affection toward one another. Maybe there are times when you wonder if you married or are dating the "right one." Your spouse or soon-to-be spouse is so much different than you are. They think, act, sleep, worship, eat, drink, love, study, drive, clean, dress, (have I said enough yet?) etc... differently than you do.

I'm sure you have heard the old axiom; "Opposites attract." But the question is, did you know that before you got married? Maybe, but most of us have never believed or accepted the fact that it could be true in our situation. Clearly we knew that on our wedding night we had just married Mr. Right or Miss Perfect. But after every wedding comes a marriage. The next morning our doubts commence to take place about our Mr. Right or Miss Perfect because suddenly our new soul mate doesn't seem to be the same person they were the day before. We had never seen them without any make up or ever dreamed they left their clothes on the floor. We discover they squeeze the toothpaste instead of rolling it. He leaves the commode lid up while she leaves hair in the sink. She's a night owl while he retires to bed early. Each passing day the doubt increases and grows. Days seem like weeks and we begin to wonder why we even married this person. They are not who we thought they were. To our amazement we discover we really have very little in common. The words, "I love you" are shared less and less. Our promised marriage partner doesn't seem to understand our inner feelings anymore. Then one morning, reality sets in. It hits like an atom bomb, because we realize our mate never talks to us anymore. And you wonder, "Why? What happened?" We know *we* haven't changed. We know *we* are still the same person we were before we got married. We hold to the belief our mate is the one who changed. Almost overnight our lifelong mate never seems to see things our way anymore. Most of us believe we are in the right and our spouse is wrong in the things that are important. And because of situations just like the above, we soon find ourselves trying to change our lifelong soul mate back to the way they were before we got married into someone better, someone just like we are. Does any of this sound familiar?

Have you ever thought of how long it is going to take to help your forever mate to see things your way? "However carefully and wisely marriage may have been entered into, few couples are completely united when the marriage ceremony is performed. *The real union of the two in wedlock is the work of the after years.*"[4]

Many couples marry believing their marriage will be a bed of roses; that love for each other is all that counts. But we have to remember that roses grow on bushes full of thorns. And often when a rose is picked, we get pricked. And what happens when we are pricked? Hurt and pain follows. Marriage can be one of thorns and thistles but also can be one of roses and violets. A well-balanced marriage is one that can adjust to the understanding that both exist. No one can have everything just like they want it. Every married person must do the best they can in making room for flexibility in their marriage. "The marriage institution was designed of Heaven to be a blessing to man; but, in a general sense, it has been abused in such a manner as to make it a dreadful curse. Most of men and women have acted, in entering the marriage relation, as though the only question for them to settle was, whether they loved each other. But they should realize that a responsibility rests upon them in the marriage relation farther than this."[5] "God does not promise us ease, honor, or wealth in His service." [6]

Confucius once said, "The grass must bend when the wind blows across it." In any marriage there will be times when we must bend, too. Being able to adjust and readjust is something that must be learned and accomplished by all who hope to have a happy home. Some things can be changed to our liking, some things cannot. And when they cannot, then we must accept the fact that any change that comes will have to come from ourselves.

Not long ago my youngest son considered getting married. I didn't think it was a good idea because he and she argued constantly. I'll never forget his words when I tried to talk to him about this. "Dad," he said, "If we get all of our arguing done now, then there won't be any after we are married!" Thank the Lord he called the wedding off!

I pray the book you hold in your hand is more than just a study on how to "learn" to have a happier marriage. Its intended use is to help you understand your soul mate in a totally new light; to accept each other for who he or she is. I hope to help you understand that no marriage partner owns the other and should never try to force personality changes. You will discover only God can bring about such changes. Each person will answer to God personally for his or her behavior. "So then every one of us shall give account of himself to God" (Romans 14:12). This book isn't written to teach you how to change your spouse into being the perfect mate, but to teach you how to become the perfect mate. You will learn only by having complete trust and confidence in each other will true happiness be found in your marriage. I hope to teach you to spend less time trying to figure out and judging your spouse, but to spend more time trying to please him or her.

This volume could be weighed like so many others as a handbook or manual on understanding why your spouse acts the way he or she does. But I pray it accomplishes much more than that. I desire it will help you uncover the truth and knowledge of how your spouse thinks and a deeper look into why he or she does what he or she does. It is my firm belief that if we know how people think, it's easier to know why their action is the way it is which often exasperates us.

This reference work will help teach you how to live happily ever after with your spouse. I will prove that by keeping your spouse happier, you will be happy also. I hope to demonstrate the secret to any successful marriage lies not in having the perfect mate, but rather in being the perfect mate.

As I stated earlier, it's no hidden secret that for years, hundreds of books have been written on how to have a happier marriage. The shelves at almost any bookstore are lined one after another with volumes guaranteeing their readers an instant solution to their marital problems. But this book takes a little different twist than the rest. It is written with the motive of regenerating any married couple into a better understanding of each other by taking a look at our different temperaments and how we tick. Then we will compare it with the truths and principles of God's Word and see what God has to say about how to have a happy, complete, and full marriage.

Throughout this publication you will find Scripture, Spirit of Prophecy quotes, examples, and personal stories. It is full of ideas and guidelines to help you really hear your spouse when he or she tries to explain why he or she does the things they do. This volume, like my book on witnessing, is not to point out who is right or wrong. It's about accepting our loved ones for who they are. Like looking through their glasses, taking a walk in their shoes, and reading their diary to understand their true deep inner feelings.

The mission of the Seventh-day Adventist Church has always been to "Go ye into all the world, and preach the gospel to every creature" Matthew 28:20. I believe this includes our homes, too. Unity and love must be found in each household in order for God to bless our home. God's plan for the Christian home is; "Marked diversities of disposition and character frequently exist in the same family, *for it is in the order of God that persons of varied temperaments should associate together*. When this is the case, each member of the household should sacredly regard the feelings and respect the right of the others. By this means mutual consideration and forbearance will be cultivated, prejudices will be softened, and rough points of character smoothed. Harmony may be secured, *and the blending of the varied temperaments may be a benefit to each other*. Christian courtesy is the golden clasp uniting the members of the family in bonds of love that become closer and stronger every day."[7]

Wow! If I understand that statement correctly, in order for our marriages to be happy, our love for one another to grow stronger to the point we become closer each day, then we must work within our own, along with our mate's temperament. It also tells me God's design for a happy home is one where opposites attract. Then our marriage is to blend together in such a way we benefit one another.

I remember when my wife and I were dating; I acted like a perfect gentleman. I said the things I thought she would want to hear. I dressed and wore the clothes I believed she would enjoy seeing me in. I sat upright at dinner without my elbows on the table. I held the fork and spoon correctly with the napkin in my lap. I didn't slurp my drink or talk with my mouth full. In other words, I was everything except the real me. Now don't misconstrue what I just said, I'm not a slob. It's just that I had placed a mask on to become the perfect polished gentleman she wanted me to be.

Well, you know what happened the day after we were married. I took the mask off and it has been down hill at full speed ever since. With each passing day the speed increased until we were about to run into the crossroads of no return. We both admit that without the grace of God holding us together those first few years, we would not be together today. *"There is not one marriage in one hundred that results happily*, that bears the sanction of God, and places the parties in a position better to glorify Him. The evil consequences of poor marriages are numberless. They are contracted from impulse."[8] We felt we were in that category.

I remember looking throughout God's Word for a loophole to leave this marriage and start over. But I soon discovered that none existed. In fact the Bible is very clear when it comes to filing for a divorce. "'Is it lawful for a man to put away his wife?' Matthew 19:3. Among the Jews a man was permitted to put away his wife for the most trivial offenses, and the woman was then at liberty to marry again. This practice led to great wretchedness and sin. In the Sermon on the Mount Jesus declared plainly that there could be no dissolution of the marriage tie, except for unfaithfulness to the marriage vow. 'Everyone,' He said, 'that putteth away his wife, saving for the cause of fornication, maketh her an adulteress: and whosoever shall marry her when she is put away committeth adultery.'"[9]

After much prayer and discussion, Kathy and I decided we were going to make our marriage work no matter what the cost. We were both convinced God brought us together and He would help keep us together. According to many of the leading authors who write about temperaments today, Kathy and I have the perfect temperament blend and match for each other. And yet we seem to constantly disagree on almost everything. Our thoughts are as different as night and day. She wants quietness when I want noise. When she wants the air conditioner on, I want the windows open for fresh air (and to save money, of course). She likes an automatic transmission; I like the stick shift. (Every man knows it's much more fun to drive a stick and it saves gas too.) We even disagree on what style of mayonnaise to purchase. She likes the real stuff and I like salad dressing. And the list continues. Almost everything in our marriage is that way. We are as opposite as two people can be. Over the years of our marriage we have learned to strengthen, enhance, magnify, and support each other within our temperaments, but only because of our decision to allow God to work in our personal lives. "Religion is needed in the home. Only this can prevent the grievous wrongs, which so often embitter married life. *Only where Christ reigns can there be deep, true, unselfish love*. Then soul will be knit with soul, *and the two lives will blend in harmony*. Angels of God will be guests in the home, and their holy vigils will hallow the marriage chamber."[10]

Why are we so different? Because our temperaments are the exact opposite! There is nothing that has a more profound influence on our behavior than our inherited temperaments. Our temperaments influence everything we do. From our sleeping habits to our eating manner, even to the way we communicate with each other. Temperaments are the combination of our parents' genes and chromosomes, which we've inherited. Conception was the most important moment of our entire life. Nine months before we even drew our first breath, God arranged our temperaments through the genes of our parents during the process of conception. It is our temperaments that make us what we are: outgoing and extrovert, or shy and introvert. I have heard it said that if a baby is a kicker in the mother's womb he will be a kicker in life. It is our temperaments, which decide whether we like art, music, sports, and even, influences our preferences to a certain color. They are largely responsible for our actions, reactions, and even to the way we emotionally respond to every situation we encounter throughout our life.

You and I are each born with certain character traits. Some of the traits are good and some not so good. In the book *Desire of Ages*, page 296, we find that we are born with "inherited…tendencies to evil." On the same page the author adds that, "By beholding Christ, they (the disciples) became transformed in character."

I have discovered through years of counseling couples and individuals that many are completely unaware their temperaments have such a powerful sway and control on their behavior. Many fight against their natural temperaments instead of cooperating with them. This often causes an inner conflict and is the very reason why we sometimes have a hard time making up our minds on some affairs and transactions. I have unearthed the truth that when you fight against your natural temperaments and try to become someone God never intended you to be, you not only cause problems in your own life, but those in your family as well.

Those of you who have read my book *Power Witnessing* will recognize some of the similarities I write in this book. Believe it or not, learning to be a good witness also applies to learning how to have a happy marriage. It has some vital information that will help you understand this book better. In it we examined this quote from *Testimonies for the Church*, vol. 4, pg. 69 in great detail. "We all need to study character and manner that we may know how to deal judiciously with different minds." We investigated how this quote could be used in our witnessing programs. In this edition we will reexamine that same statement only this time in the scope of marriage and explore this charge: "To gain a proper understanding of the marriage relation *is the work of a lifetime.*"[11] "Work of a lifetime!" Ouch! Is it starting to become clear why we can't always seem to communicate to our spouse our true inner thoughts, feelings, and needs? Just like "Sanctification is not a work of a day or a year, but of a lifetime."[12] So is learning how to have a happy marriage.

We will also look at why it's easier to understand why we do the things we do, than it is to understand why our spouse, children and others act the way they do.

Throughout this book we will glance at different temperament blends and matches. I believe you will find God knows what He is doing when He brings two people together who think totally opposite of each other.

I personally believe each married person can have a happier marriage if they will learn to accept their mate with the God given temperaments, talents, and gifts they have.

Since God doesn't make mistakes at birth, He gave each of us the perfect temperament blend He knew we would want and need. During my seminars I often ask the question if anyone would like to have a different temperament than what they have been born with? Almost everyone says no. There have been a few melancholies (mostly ladies) who mention they would like to have a little more sanguine temperament in them but also keep the temperament they have. They want to have fun but at the same time be perfect. Can you do that?

Some might question why another book on marriage? Isn't there enough already? Listen to these words. "Doctrinal discourses have been preached to the people, and many have listened and have accepted the doctrines, who have had little knowledge of the word of God; for they have not been students of the Bible, and have never felt it their duty to dig deep in the mines of truth. They catch at the surface truths. A much more thorough work should be done. *Some system must be adopted, that those who really want to know the truth as it is in Jesus*, may have an opportunity of becoming students, and that they may seek earnestly for spiritual knowledge and understanding, and partake of the rich provision of the Master's table."[13] If we really want to learn how to have a happier marriage, then each of us will have to search the Scriptures and see what God says we must do when two become one. Adopting new ideas is not usually easy, but if we allow God to lead and show us His plan and design for us as individuals and as a married couple, then we will find blessings and happiness we never knew existed.

In following these simple steps, guidelines, and principles you'll find in this book, your marriage can become happier. But it will take time and work on your part. What you will learn in this book is not some recent discovery on how to have a happier marriage. It is not some new theology or theory. It's been around ever since God first made mankind. It has always been Gods plan for us to love, accept, and understand our spouse and family.

What you read in this volume is not to be used as a crutch or excuse for ourselves concerning why we do certain things the way we do. It is to help you understand why *your mate* does the things they do; to encourage you to learn the right words and behavior so that others will be able to understand better as you communicate your feelings and as they communicate theirs.

I'm praying this book will help you accept the fact God brought you and your spouse together and by coming to a better understanding of your temperament, your marriage can be fun, exciting, and promising. I hope you will be motivated and inspired to try courting all over again. And above all, I pray by the time you are through reading this book, you and your spouse will have developed a closer relationship with Jesus.

It doesn't matter if you have been married for a week or fifty years, this reference work can and will help you. Even if you just want to improve your marriage or trying to survive a dead marriage, you'll find help and support. Many of the principles you find in this book have worked for my wife and me for years. I pray they will work for you, too. I urge you to join me in using examples from our Bible, the Spirit of Prophecy and life experiences in developing a closer relationship with Jesus as we *"Learn to Live Happily Ever After."*

Chapter 1

"Learning to Live Happily Ever After"

As I look back on it now, it was sort of funny how I asked Kathy to marry me. We had been dating for several months and not a day would roll by that we didn't spend some time with each other. Even while at work at night, I would call her at her home just to see what she and Tonya, her daughter, were doing.

Kathy and I worked for the same man that owned two restaurants that were beside each other. I worked a split shift, 9:00 AM to 1:00 PM and then returned at 5:00 and worked to closing time. Between my work shifts, I often would pick Tonya up from her grandmother's house and keep her for the afternoon until Kathy got off at 5:00 PM. But this afternoon would be different. We weren't going to the park or riding around, I had another plan, a plan I shared with little six-year-old Tonya.

Because I had been raised a Seventh-day Adventist, and had now been attending church again for several months, I remembered Adventists believe what the Bible teaches concerning jewelry. (At least they believed in 1979. Today I sometimes wonder). When I grew up we were taught to obey what God says in 1 Timothy 2:9 and 1 John 2:15–17; "In like manner also, that women adorn themselves in modest apparel, with shamefacedness and sobriety; not with braided hair, or gold, or pearls, or costly array." "Love not the world, neither the things that are in the world. If any man love the world, the love of the Father is not in him. For all that is in the world, the lust of the flesh, and the lust of the eyes, and the pride of life, is not of the Father, but is of the world. And the world passeth away, and the lust thereof: but he that doeth the will of God abideth for ever." So I came up with the plan to ask Kathy to marry me using a watch.

Tonya and I visited a local jewelry store where she helped me pick out a nice watch costing $100.00. It had two "huge" diamonds on the side of the band that you needed a strong magnifying glass to see. (Huge is the word the jeweler used, anyway). I had it gift-wrapped and was so proud of myself. It wasn't until later that afternoon before I thought, what if she says "no." What then? It took some time and coaching from Tonya for me to muster up enough courage to go ahead with my plan, but I finally did.

I walked into Pizza Inn where Kathy was working and found her doing her usual duty for that time of day vacuuming the floor. Since it was 3:00 in the afternoon, and no one eats pizza at that time of day, the dining room was empty. I asked her if she would stop for a moment because I had something I wanted to ask her. As she was putting the vacuum cleaner away, I asked the cook if he would mind watching Tonya since I had something very important to ask Kathy. Since Tonya was in on the plan she told the cook she would tell him all about it.

When we sat down my heart was pounding ninety-miles-a-minute. I handed Kathy the beautiful gift-wrapped box and asked her to open it. When she finished opening the box and was about to try the watch on, I said, "Kathy, it's asking you a question." She said, "What? What time is it?" I have to admit it was one of the few times this sanguine didn't know what to say. I just about lost what little courage I had left. I finally said, "No. It's asking you to marry me." Later I found out she knew all along what I was about to ask. She just wanted to see me squirm.

That was February, 1979. We were married May 27, 1979 and we are still together today. Whenever we visit that same Pizza Inn today we still call that booth, "our booth." Kathy had one of her wedding showers there and we have celebrated several of our anniversaries there always trying to sit at "our booth."

Chapter 1

Today, twenty-plus years later, we are still happily married. It's not that we haven't had our share of disagreements. We have had more than our share. (So we feel). But we have grown to love each other more and more each day. Even though our temperaments are exact opposite, and we seldom see things eye to eye, we still love each other with a commitment that's strong and feel our marriage was made in heaven. Even with our ups and down, and if the truth is to be said, we probably have had more downs than ups, we are still committed to each other. Those first few years of our marriage were rough to say the least. To this day, how the phenomenon of two people who are so opposite from each other can still have the kind of love we have is beyond my comprehending. Only a God of power and love could have performed the miracles, which have kept us together through the years.

How could we still be together with all the ups and downs we have had? There is only one simple answer. We have dedicated our lives to God and to each other. We have allowed God to attract us to the temperament combination that complements our own. As you read this book you will soon discover that the old saying "opposites attract," is true. Kathy and I are living proof to the fact. Kathy being a melancholy/choleric and me a sanguine/phlegmatic means we are the perfect union. Listen to one author's view about this perfect temperament combination that Kathy and I have. "This combination (*sanguine/phlegmatic*) brings the most lovable and possibly most easy-to-like personality (*that's me*) together with the most serious-minded (*that's my wife*) of all temperaments (*melancholy/choleric*)."[1] Can you see now how different we are?

The key to Kathy's and my marriage is our mutual growth with one another and God. We try to spend time with each other every day. We write love notes to each other and try to leave them in places we hope the other will find them. We purposely do small things for the other knowing it is something they would enjoy and appreciate. Also we try to encourage one another. Here is the blueprint for a happy home. "It is the duty of every married couple to studiously avoid marring the feelings of each other. They should control every look and expression of fretfulness and passion. *They should study each other's happiness, in small matters, as well as in large*, manifesting a tender thoughtfulness, in acknowledging kind acts and the little courtesies of each other. These small things should not be neglected, for they are just as important to the happiness of man and wife, as food is necessary to sustain physical strength. The father should encourage wife and mother to lean upon his large affections. Kind, cheerful, encouraging words from him with whom she has entrusted her life happiness, will be more beneficial to her than any medicine; and the cheerful rays of light which such sympathizing words will bring to the heart of the wife and mother, will reflect back their own cheering beams upon the heart of the father."[2]

Long ago Kathy and I encountered having a happy home goes way beyond telling each other, "I love you." It goes way beyond expressing how much we need and want the other. Having a happy family has to start with having Christ as our helper. *"Men and women can reach God's ideal for them if they will take Christ as their helper*. What human wisdom cannot do, His grace will accomplish for those who give themselves to Him in loving trust. His providence can unite hearts in bonds that are of heavenly origin. Love will not be a mere exchange of soft and flattering words… The result is not a tissue fabric, but a texture that will bear wear and test and trial. Heart will be bound to heart in the golden bonds of a love that is enduring."[3]

Because our temperaments are so different, we often find it hard to explain to the other how we really feel inside on various issues. This has caused many misunderstandings throughout our married life. Then there have been times when we wore a mask trying to hide our true inner feelings. As you will see later in this book, wearing a mask in front of others is much easier for some temperaments than for others.

Chapter 1

In the 1998 fourth quarter Sabbath School Guide, I read a good illustration taken from the book *Let Me Illustrate* by author Donald Grey Barnhouse on how we can better study to understand our spouse. It went something like this.

"Several centuries ago, the Emperor of Japan commissioned a Japanese artist to paint a bird. Months passed, then years. Finally, the Emperor went to the artist's studio to ask for an explanation. The artist set a blank canvas on the easel and in fifteen minutes completed the painting of a bird that became a masterpiece. The Emperor asked why there had been such a long delay. The artist then...produced armloads of drawings of feathers, tendons, wings, feet, claws, eyes and beaks of birds; these he placed one by one before the Emperor."[4]

That illustration is a good example of how long it takes us to study our mate. It takes time. Much time. In fact it's the work of a lifetime. This reminds me of Galatians 4:19: "My little children, of whom I travail in birth again until Christ be formed in you." We need to understand and accept the fact that our mates are not perfect and will never be in this lifetime. When we understand and accept that fact, then we will find our marriages much happier. This is why it is so important to treat our loved ones with respect and kindness. You can never take back a wrong you have done to your spouse. "A wrong act can never be undone. It may be that the *work of a lifetime* will not recover what has been lost in a single moment of temptation or even thoughtlessness."[5] "Remember, it would take the work of a lifetime to recover what a moment of yielding to temptation and thoughtlessness throws away."[6] If we will take that into consideration each time we are tempted to speak rashly, then we might find ourselves hurting each other less.

Shortly after Kathy and I were married I discovered she didn't enjoy the same things I did. I enjoy camping in the great outdoors, but Kathy's idea of roughing it is going to a Motel Six and discovering the swimming pool is closed. She likes soft music where as I enjoy music with a toe-tapping beat. Everything that we seemed to enjoy and talked about before we were married seemed to change overnight. Kathy thought I had lied and tricked her, and I guess I felt the same way about her. So what did we do about it? We did what almost every red-blooded newly wedded couple does. We tried to change the other into someone they're not: someone similar to ourselves. Needless to say, it did not work. We both dug our heels in and would not give an inch. Her choleric temperament and my phlegmatic temperament both came to the surface. As you will soon discover, both of these temperament traits can be headstrong and stubborn. And even though these are our secondary temperaments, when it comes to standing our grounds, they come to the surface and we won't budge!

But over the years, through trial and error, mistakes and misunderstanding, hurt and disappointments, we came to the understanding that because God made us the way we are, we have no business trying to change the other. Now that isn't to say we do not try to help the other see themselves at times, but we have come to a better understanding of why we each do what we do.

As I stated earlier, *"To gain a proper understanding of the marriage relation is the work of a lifetime.* Those who marry enter a school from which they are never in this life to be graduated."[7]

If the way to having a happier marriage is the work of a lifetime, then why is it that fifty-percent of all marriage partners have flunked and quit school? Isn't it crystal-clear that every Christian's duty is to study their spouse's temperament to determine what it will take to make them happy? We must work everyday, every minute toward understanding their likes and dislikes and why. Then and only then will any of us have the complete and happy marriage God planned for us to have in the beginning.

If you read my first book you may remember the illustration I gave on how we cannot throw an effective witnessing program together in five minutes. It takes time putting together a program that will work effectively. Well, the same example applies to having a happy home. Expecting to throw together an energetic happy marriage without working at it is impossible. It takes time, energy, and much prayer. *"The precious graces of the Holy Spirit are not developed in a moment.* Courage, fortitude, meekness, faith, unwavering trust in God's power to save, *are acquired by the experience of years.* By a life of holy endeavor and firm adherence to the right the children of God are to seal their destiny."[8]

I truly believe that for any marriage to be happy, we must accept our mate for who and what they are without any restrictions. "We differ so widely in disposition, habits, education, that our ways of looking at things vary. We judge differently. Our understanding of truth, our ideas in regard to the conduct of life, are not in all respects the same. *There are no two whose experience is alike in every particular.* The trials of one are not the trials of another. The duties that one finds light, are to another most difficult and perplexing."[9]

It is my personal conviction that unless we learn to accept our mates for who they are, we will never experience the happiness Jesus has for us. I wouldn't be writing this book if I didn't hold this belief with full confidence. The closer we get to the Second Coming, the more we must accept the fact that no two people think or act identically. Understanding the temperament theory, I believe, is one way for having a happy and complete marriage. This concept isn't perfect, but in my view, it can be a very helpful tool in understanding human behavior. It is not accepted universally, but if used in its right perspective, it will be an excellent aid and guidance to why your spouse acts the way he or she does. I pray that before you are through reading this book, you will have a better understanding of your lifetime soul mate.

Chapter 2

"What are Temperaments?"

If a church could be considered a hospital for sinners, then couldn't a marriage be considered a home for lovers? "Let each give love rather than exact it. Cultivate that which is noblest in yourselves, and be quick to recognize the good qualities in each other. The consciousness of being appreciated is a wonderful stimulus and satisfaction. Sympathy and respect encourage the striving after excellence, and love itself increases as it stimulates to nobler aims.... Love will not be a mere exchange of soft and flattering words. The loom of heaven weaves with warp and woof finer, yet more firm, than can be woven by the looms of earth. The result is not a tissue fabric, but a texture that will bear wear and test and trial. Heart will be bound to heart in the golden bonds of a love that is enduring.

"Better than gold is a peaceful home,

Where all the fireside charities come;

The shrine of love and the heaven of life,

Hallowed by mother, or sister, or wife.

However humble the home may be,

Or tried with sorrows by heaven's decree,

The blessings that never were bought or sold,

And center there, are better than gold."[1]

Have you ever wondered why it is that the majority of people we associate with seem to behave and think totally different than you do? It's as if the vast preponderance of those we are in contact with act and voice things we would never even think of. Have you ever noticed that some people never seem to shed their bad habits? Day in and day out they do and say the same old things that either hurt or disappoint us. Has it ever bothered you that some Christians rarely express the words, "I'm sorry," for their bad behavior even though they themselves might call it sin? It doesn't matter how much they have hurt you or someone else, voicing those words is next to impossible for them. On the other hand, another Christian may say they're sorry and ask for forgiveness for the same mistake seventy times seven. They may appear sincere in asking you to pray in their behalf appealing for victory, but from what you can see, victory never comes. The very next day they do the exact same sinful habit that again has hurt and disappointed you. Nothing changed. And you wonder why, Lord, why?

Let's talk about compulsive emotions and behavior for a moment. Today I understand better than ever why human beings become enslaved to what psychologists call, obsessive-compulsive behavior. Through the course of my studies in psychology of what makes a human tick, I've uncovered the fact that every person's, both *good* and *bad* qualities, are established and determined by the temperament traits they were born with. This may not come as a shock to you, but to those of us who didn't have psychology in high school, it might. It sure did me. It wasn't until I was studying for my Masters in psychology that I came across this amazing discovery of temperaments. In fact the temperament philosophy was totally new to me. At first I wondered how many others knew about this extraordinary hypothesis of understanding people's behavior and deportment. I came to find that many people have little or no knowledge of the four basic personality types: melancholy, phlegmatic, sanguine, and choleric. It was for this very reason I attempted my first publication, *Power Witnessing, How to Reach Different Personalities for Christ* and the manuscript you hold.

Probably the greatest shock of my life came when *Review and Herald* informed me they had accepted my proposed book and wanted to publish the research I had done on how to witness to people. In it I attempted to prove that if we witness to others in *their* temperament, *not our own*, we will see more souls won for Jesus.

My research came from a course in my Masters in Christian Counseling Psychology. The course required I read and study the book, *Personality Plus* by Florence Littauer. While studying this book, I was introduced to the temperament theory. Her book made me rethink everything I knew on why people do what they do.

Although not as distinguished as in melancholies, phlegmatics also have an analytical side. They rely heavily on data, analysis, and logic to make important decisions. They like to thoroughly examine and study people's needs and situations. Well, with phlegmatic being my secondary temperament, I quickly started analyzing and breaking down everything about my life and those around me. Some things I liked, some things I didn't.

It wasn't long until I found myself taking a survey of my personal one-on-one Bible studies and how I witnessed. It was then I made a phenomenal discovery. Every soul I had ever won to Jesus through one-on-one Bible Studies were of the same temperament as myself. They were all sanguines and a few phlegmatics. I questioned, "Why is that?" I viewed the ones I could not persuade to make a decision for Christ, and I realized they were of a totally different temperament than myself. Then it came into full view what I had done. I had studied with others in *my* temperament, not theirs. What I did was try to convince people to see God's Word from a totally different perspective than what they were able to. I wanted everyone to understand the Bible from a sanguine's point of view. Today I realize this is next to impossible to accomplish.

Psychologists today know it's our temperaments that influence the things we do every moment of our life. From the way we sit, eat, sleep, walk, talk, dress, and comb our hair. (Sorry men, I haven't found anything yet that said temperaments have anything to do with whether you have hair or not, although it appears that extroverts seem to lose their hair sooner than introverts do). Temperaments even have a great influence on the way we communicate to our kids, spouse, and friends.

Temperaments are the combination of traits we inherited at conception from our parents. Our temperaments influence and often determine our behavior in the way we react to different situations. They also establish whether we will be outgoing and extrovert or shy and introvert. It is the temperaments that influence what sort of music or sports we enjoy.

Leading writers on psychology formulate that there is nothing more powerful and has more influence on a person's general all around make up than their temperament blend. It's our temperaments that make us feel a certain way about anything. One author put it this way. "We all need to study character and manner that we may know how to deal judiciously with different minds... The person must be shown his true character, understand his own peculiarities of disposition and temperament, and see his infirmities."[2] I believe this encompasses our marriage partner too. Every married person must have a clear understanding of how their spouse's mind thinks in order to understand why he or she behaves and acts the way they do.

There is nothing that answers questions better on why our spouse does what he or she does than the comprehension of the theory of the four temperaments. By knowing and understanding them you'll have a clearer understanding of your spouse's taste in dress, food, creative capabilities, cars, and their attitude about anything. A person's temperaments explain why some have conflict with others while at the same time are attracted to another.

At this point, let us take a quick glance over the four basic temperaments so that from here on out you'll have a clearer picture of the temperament theory as we continue *Learning How to Live Happily Ever After*.

Chapter 3

"University of Hard Knocks"

Have you ever felt like a graduate from the "University of Hard Knocks in Marriage" with a Ph.D. in "Blunders" as your major? You took all the advance courses that were offered in "Stupid Mistakes." You graduated highest in your class and now would like to submit your resume' with the local university seeking the position of professor.

Over the course of my studies and life experiences, I've discovered that no two people think or behave the exact same way. Not married couples, children, family, or friends. "The laws of genetics have reported that there are 300 billion possible chromosome combinations for human beings."[1] This means it is relatively impossible that two people could be the same. Each of us is truly one of a kind. Individuals are as different as snowflakes and fingerprints. In the beginning our Lord designed that each individual was to have certain strengths in his or her temperament and character. After sin came into this world so did the weaknesses that blemished our temperament and character. "Sin entered this world, and by yielding to the temptations of the enemy, man became degraded and sinful. His ability to distinguish between right and wrong was lost; his power to obey was weakened."[2] "When man sinned, his nature became evil, and he was in harmony, and not at variance, with Satan."[3] Because sin entered into the human race, we now have major defects and blemishes in our behavior and character. I believe that is why some people can do something that thrills them one moment and then put it to death the next. This explains why we sometimes admire a part of a person's character and be perturbed and agitated with another part.

No doubt many of you have heard of Oscar Schindler. A few years back a huge box office hit was entitled, *Schindler's List*. It was the amazing story about a German who used his wealth and wiles to rescue 1,200 Polish Jews during World War II. It was a humane and noble effort. I watched the video and the ending showed hundreds of people, who had been saved because of his undertaking, standing around his grave giving him honor.

But what astonished me was to hear in a sermon what *U.S. News and World Report* published about him after the war. This once brave and noble patriot ended up abandoning his wife, becoming a womanizer and a drunkard. He lived his last days in destitution and total dependence upon others. So far did he fall that he took the very ring that had been fashioned for him (from the gold harvested from the teeth of the people he rescued,) and pawned it for a bottle of schnapps. Of course the movie didn't show this.

I couldn't help but wonder how could this be? How could someone so noble and heroic fall so far? Again I believe it's because of sin entering into the human race 6,000 years ago, causing the weakness in our temperaments; thus making our character and personality do what we do—good or bad.

"The religion we profess is colored by our natural dispositions and temperaments; therefore, it is of the *highest importance* that the *weak points* in our character be *strengthened* by exercise and that the strong, unfavorable *points be weakened by working in an opposite direction* and by strengthening opposite qualities."[4]

We humans have the tendency to work on our weak points of character instead of our strengths. But we need to strengthen our weak points by simply working on our strong points. In other words, if we work on our strong points of character, the weak points will take care of themselves and become weaker and weaker until they fade out of sight.

Growing up in west Texas, I developed a very noticeable Texas accent. I also picked up all the slang and bad grammar, which comes along with growing up in the Lone Star State. Needless to say, when I started preaching, many of the English majors quickly started correcting my grammar. (They couldn't help me with my accent.) To correct this problem I started listening and studying how proper English grammar is to be used. Kathy was (and still is) a tremendous help in this area also. Today, although I still have a way to go, I can at times speak and preach without having the grammar majors shiver with every other word that comes from my lips. They hear my message instead of my syntax.

How did I do this? How did my grammar go from shocking to pleasing? Simply by studying the proper way to speak instead of searching for the improper grammar I used. In other words, I worked in the opposite direction. This is what strengthened my weakness. The same example holds true for the person who works at a bank searching for counterfeit money. They spend their time studying the true instead of looking at the false.

I believe this rule applies for marriages, too. When we uncover the strengths and weaknesses of our own, along with that of our spouse's temperament, we unearth what makes us tick and how we think. Then hopefully we can apply this knowledge in such a way that we better understand how to communicate with each other.

I am writing this book with the notion you might have some background with the four basic temperaments, - sanguine, choleric, melancholy, and phlegmatic. But since I don't know for sure, please allow me to explain a little more about something that each one of us has; our own unique and personal temperament.

When we talk about temperaments you must first understand that they are what influence and determine why we behave the way we do, from the way we communicate with others to the profession we choose. Temperaments play a huge role in the books we read and sway in how we

Chapter 3

discipline and treat our children. Temperaments hold an enormous sway on how we conduct our married life. In other words, temperaments determine everything we do!

One point that needs to be made here is the fact that our temperaments never change. We may try to change the color of our skin like Michael Jackson did. We may have the ability to change our hair-do and regulate our body from fat to thin. We can wear high heel shoes to make us look taller and make-up to hide the blemishes. We can do whatever we want with the outside of our bodies that others see, but our true temperament, our ticking clock which makes us who we are on the inside, never changes.

During some of my seminars on the temperament theory, I've had a few people try to convince me that their temperament changed as they got older. But this is not the case. What happens is with each indoctrination of our life, with each book we read or don't read, every program we watch on television, the friends we associate with; each determines how our personality or character is formed. But our true temperament never changes.

Let me see if I can explain what I mean. Your temperament is the traits or general makeup of who you are. You were born with your temperament. It is genetic and you had no control on what your temperament would be. Just like you had no control on whom your parents would be. But your character is the real you. It is the result of your natural temperament modified by all outside influences. Everything we do or don't do makes up our character.

Our personality is our outward expression. It is the face we choose to show the world. The Latin word *persona*, which means "A mask worn by actors," best describes our personality. When I preach, I have on my preacher mask. When I drive, I have on my driving mask. Right now you are reading my writer's mask. When I'm around my wife, I have on my husband mask. I let people see the person I want them to see.

Let's face it. No one knows the real you. My wife, children, closest and dearest friends do not know the real me. I only let them see what I allow them to see. But now and then I do slip up and let people see more of my other side than I intend to. This is when I get some of the funniest looks. My wife doesn't hesitate to inform me of my childish behavior. As you will soon read, we sanguines never grow up and often act like big children.

Right after Kathy and I were married we would often take a trip and visit with my family. Shortly after we would begin our trip home Kathy would inform me that I had embarrassed her with the way I acted. What actually happened was she saw more of the real me. Around my family I had taken off my "Kathy's husband mask." She didn't like what she saw. This is not uncommon in many marriages. I frequently hear the same protest from other married couples. Kathy will tell you she doesn't act the same at her family's home as she does at ours.

Let me give you another example. Have you ever wondered why your spouse will eat or drink something totally different while visiting someone but would never think about eating or drinking it at home? At home you see the real person while the host is seeing a mask they are wearing. Have you ever told someone they looked nice or that you enjoyed the dish they just served you when in truth you felt differently? Sure, we all have at one time or another.

I recall before I became a pastor, I would often tell my minister, as I shook his hand at the door, that I received a huge blessing from his sermon. Then I would repeat the same words the next Sabbath. The truth is, I didn't always receive a "huge" blessing. Yes I would receive a blessing but not always as large a blessing as I would let on. Just being at church and fellowshipping with others would bring me a warm feeling that was a "huge" blessing.

I remember the minister that re-baptized me and later married Kathy and me. I consider him a good pastor, but I didn't always understand his sermons. When trying to explain the Word of God he often spoke way over my head.

Chapter 3

This was because his temperament is completely different from mine. When he preached in his temperament it was very difficult for me to follow him. God nevertheless used this man to bring me back to Him.

Today, years later, I have many church members tell me they enjoyed and received a blessing from my sermon most every week. (For some reason they don't use the word "huge.") I know now that not every sermon I preach will be a blessing to every person because I preach with my sanguine style temperament. I use many stories and illustrations to open up windows. This style of preaching doesn't appeal to everyone because I've had members ask me to use more scripture and fewer stories. Others have asked me to stay behind the pulpit and not walk around so much. Some have asked me not to use so much hand motion. So I know that not everyone receives a "huge" blessing every week. Nevertheless, most members still put on the happy "That's a good sermon mask" and do the Christian thing by telling me they received a blessing.

The foundation of this book is not to point out who's right or who's wrong in our marriages. It is about learning why our spouse and children do what they do. It is to unearth the reasons why our spouse can please us one moment and irritate us the next. It is to take a walk in their shoes and look through their eyes. To be able to open up their heart, see what makes them tick, and discover what they look like under their mask.

The study of the four basic temperaments is not a new theology. It's been around since before Christ came the first time. We should only use it as a tool that will help us understand how different minds think.

It is not my purpose to write another book about marriage, but rather to underscore the things we already know about marriage. I'd like to prove that attending the "University of Hard Knocks" has its advantages as long as we learn from our mistakes. Someone once said: "Wise is the one who learns from their mistakes, but wiser is the one who learns from someone else's mistakes." We all make mistakes, but the wise among us are less apt to make the same mistake the second time. "For I have learned by experience…" Genesis 30:27. Percy Bysshe Shelley said; "If life had a second edition, how I would correct the proofs."

In spite of all the mistakes and mishaps we place ourselves into, one thing is in our favor and that is, God has given us the ability to learn from them. To learn from our mistakes is a huge blessing! We are in school being educated each moment of our life. Take advantage of it now, because if you don't, then you will surely have to later.

What I want to share with you throughout this entire volume is that our marriage can be better understood than previously. "There is a science of Christianity to be mastered,—a science as much deeper, broader, higher than any human science as the heavens are higher than the earth. The mind is to be disciplined, educated, trained; for we are to do service for God in ways that are not in harmony with inborn inclination. There are hereditary and cultivated tendencies to evil that must be overcome. Often the training and education of a lifetime must be discarded that one may become a learner in the school of Christ. Our hearts must be educated to become steadfast in God. We are to form habits of thought that will enable us to resist temptation. We must learn to look upward. The principles of the word of God—principles that are as high as heaven, and that compass eternity—we are to understand in their bearing upon our daily life. Every act, every word, every thought, is to be in accord with these principles."[5]

Chapter 4

"Lord Have Mercy, I Married a Motor-Mouth Joker: *The Sanguine*"

"God's way is to give man something he has not... to make man something he is not. Man's way is to get an easy place,... and selfish ambition. God's plan is to set man to work in reformatory lines; then he will learn by experience how long he has pampered fleshly appetites, and ministered to his own temperament, bringing weakness upon himself.

"God's way is to work in power... Man is too often satisfied to treat himself according to the methods of quackery, and he vindicates his manner of working as right. God proposes to purify and refine the defiled soul; then he will implant in the heart his own righteousness and peace and health, and man becomes complete in him. Then the issues of life, proceeding from the heart, are represented as a well of water, springing up into everlasting life."[1]

Years ago I received a call to pastor a district in Iowa. The three-church district consisted of Ft. Dodge, Lake City, and Boone. We met many lovely people and enjoyed our three years there immensely. I grew up in the south where if it does snow, it is usually gone within a few days. There in Iowa, it snowed and stayed for what seemed forever. I had heard of cabin fever before, but I thought it was nothing more than a myth. But by the time that third winter rolled in on us, I was experiencing it badly. This was when my wife really started discovering my personality flaws. (As if she hadn't already). I became cocky, touchy, and opinionated. I became irritated very easily and was constantly edgy. It's always been hard for me to take constructive criticism, but at this point in my life complaining from anyone revealed a side of me no one (not even me) knew existed. I had become a full-blown gripe-a-holic and a flat-out grumpy old man.

In the next four chapters you will learn a lot about my family and me. Our family unit makes up each one of the four temperaments. We are what you might call a "complete temperament family blend." I have asked each one their permission to use many of their life experiences to describe each of the four basic temperaments. Since I'm the sanguine of the family, and we sanguines always like being first, I will start with and "pick" on myself here at the beginning.

I once saw a television commercial showing a man on the high diving board. His dive was to be judged for his performance and exhibition. As he approached the end of the board he stumbled causing him to somersault as he left the plank. On his way down, he tried his best to correct the dive. When he finally came up out of the water he was yelling, "Yes, yes, a perfect dive!" While at the same time the judges were holding up cards, which read, 0.0, 0.0, 0.0. In others words, they gave him a big fat zero for his performance while the young man thought he had done extraordinarily fantastic. To make it simple, that is a perfect example of your incredible everyday sanguine!

A sanguine is the happy, enthusiastic, bubbly, joyful, care-free, talkative companion who never knows when or how to shut-up. They're the husband or wife who is never embarrassed to tell everyone how great a person they are. They love to talk about their number one fan – themselves. They feel they are the best lovers on the earth and like to be very romantic. They give credence to the fact that they could write a book (11,025 and ½ pages long) on how to be the greatest intimate mate. Because of all their self-complacency in themselves, however, their spouse often becomes confused because they may not think they are that great a lover. (But never tell that to a sanguine, it will destroy their incredibly high self-esteem).

I wish I didn't have to write this about myself, but many of my natural feelings are just like what you read above. It's as

Chapter 4

instinctive to me as a bee is attracted to a flower; as a bear is in love with honey; and as a bird knows it must fly south for the winter. I heard a true story once about this mother hen that was sitting on her eggs, and the farmer wanted to play a dirty trick on her. He wanted to see what would happen if he placed a duck egg under her, too. So he did, and soon the chicks and duckling were hatched. Mama hen did next what came natural for chicken mothers to do, she started training the little duckling and his brothers and sisters to scratch and peck. The duckling's web feet and rounded beak didn't do quit as well as his siblings, but he managed. It wasn't long until mother was taking her family for a walk when they passed a small pond. When the baby duck saw water for the first time in his life, nature took its course, and the little duck made a mad dash for a quick swim. This didn't set too lightly with mother hen. She squawked, cackled, clucked, and used all sorts of bad chicken language that I can't write and still keep this a Christian book. She tried to persuade, with all her might, that her baby needed to get out of the water. The little duckling however, knew he was where he was supposed to be.

Temperaments are just like that. Just like a duck is naturally attracted to water, temperaments are a natural part of our make-up. As a bird's instinct tells it when to fly south for the winter, our temperaments govern the way we are controlled. We feel the way our temperament tells us to feel. We can't do a thing about the way we naturally feel inside. We can, on the other hand, do something about the way we react to that feeling.

Although I have the natural desire to brag and boast about how great I am all the time, I try with God's grace to keep it under control. I have to constantly be on guard though. This is where the born-again experience comes in for a sanguine. Keep in mind that it never comes easy for a sanguine to be humble. He or she has to depend on the Lord to show when and how to be lowly and meek.

Sanguines are super extroverts that have the instinctive desire to always be the center of attention. They can never go anywhere unnoticed. They're often found to be very enthusiastic, spirited, carefree, and a wisecrack type person. They can be very unpredictable and you never know what they might say next. I often embarrass my wife when we are in public. She becomes very nervous when she sees I'm about to open my mouth and say something. I used to think she was the only one who felt that way about us sanguines. Then after surveying other temperaments, I've discovered that many spouses of sanguines tell me, they too, become nervous and apprehensive when they see their spouse about to speak.

Both sanguines and melancholies experience the richest emotions of the four basic temperaments with a compassionate and sensitive side that often comes to view. I have the hardest time preaching sermons without getting teary. I really do not like this side of me that comes out almost every Sabbath. Not only is it embarrassing to myself, it bothers my wife also. As you will later see, phlegmatics and cholerics (hers and my secondary temperaments) do not like to see or hear people weep. Phlegmatics and cholerics feel lamenting is a sign of weakness. Hearing or seeing someone shed tears makes them feel very uncomfortable. So when my sanguine side gets teary and becomes emotional, my phlegmatic side tells me to "Get a life."

Sanguines make good marriage partners if they will learn not to take over every conversation. I don't mean to, but it seems that whenever my wife and I come in contact with someone, I feel I must lead in the discussion. This, needless to say, agitates and annoys my wife. I love to tell stories, which isn't bad in itself but most of my tales become a little lengthy resulting in never giving my wife time to speak. We sanguines also enjoy telling the same story over and over. With every time the story is recounted, the facts change a little. The story is never the same. You see, we sanguines enjoy embellishing the stories we tell. Since we like to brag about everything, this often causes great stress with our spouse, and they become humiliated. We also have the tendency to talk about family secrets that should be kept

Chapter 4

quiet. This causes even more problems at home if your spouse is not a sanguine. The other three temperaments like to keep family secrets a secret. The sanguine feels different. He or she wants the whole world to know what is happening behind their closed doors. Why do they feel that way? The answer is simple: It's another story to tell!

Sanguines are also very touching people, which would not be bad in itself, but because sanguines are at times (OK most of the time) what many call, airheads, we have the tendency to place our hands where they do not belong. I have to constantly be on guard where my hands go if I happen to pat someone on the back, which I often do. Many people like to be touched. It's a sign someone cares. But no one enjoys being touched or touching more than a sanguine! Be careful, for some sanguines might misinterpret the touch.

You no doubt have heard the "Stupid dumb blond jokes" before. You probably have also seen the television programs where the dumb blond woman makes many foolish, half-witted, and moronic mistakes time and time again. Look at her temperament, and you will see she is impersonating a sanguine. Now before I get myself into trouble, not all blond sanguine women are like that. It's just one of those "labels" they have been tagged with. A sanguine can have any color of hair and still act that way.

Since sanguines like to talk, they're never in need of a friend. We'll dialogue with anyone who will listen. If we cannot find someone to listen, we'll simply talk to ourselves. While driving alone I often receive funny looks when someone sees me talking to myself. This is one of the reasons I took up the art of ventriloquism. Now I can talk to myself, and no one sees my lips move. Ha! And they call us sanguines "half-witted." Someone once said this about a sanguine, "They always enter a room mouth first." I wish I could understand what they mean by that statement.

Unless something distressing has happened in a sanguine's life, you will almost always find them in a merry, sparkling, friendly, considerate, high-spirited, and humorous mood. If something disturbing has happened in their life, it appears God gave them the easiest and fastest temperament to bounce back into their old fun-loving self. It's hard for a sanguine to stay down and be sad. He or she enjoys having fun too much to continue being discouraged, disheartened, and depressed for any length of time. This confuses the other three temperaments. They cannot comprehend how anyone can spring back from a disaster or tragedy as fast as a sanguine can. This is one reason why sanguines don't appear to spend much time in mourning after a spouse has passed away before they are looking for another. I've often made the joke with Kathy that if anything should happen to her, that shortly after my attenuated mourning stage of a week, I would be looking for another wife. Of course she knows I'm only kidding. It would more likely be a month than a week!

As you probably realize by now, all temperaments have both strengths and weaknesses. A sanguine's quota of weaknesses runs high. (According to some.) To a sanguine, his or her weaknesses only make the day more enjoyable. Probably their greatest weakness is their unfortunate lack of discipline. This often makes trouble in many marriages because they appear to be deceptive and unreliable. They have the unsuccessful tendency to make-up a story or exaggerate the truth to keep them out of trouble. Because they often stretch the truth, when the fabrication comes into full view, their spouse believes they lied. To the sanguine however, he or she hasn't lied; they only told enough of the story to keep them out of trouble. (They hope). Unfortunately, this doesn't work very often. The other temperaments catch on quickly that there is probably more or less to the story than what has been told. We sanguines however never give up the hope that it will work the next time.

Another unlucky downside is that sanguines are extremely emotional. They're often hurt and crushed from harsh or rash words, especially from their spouse or parents. They have a very difficult time handling the thought that they have disappointed anyone. They want and need the approval of everyone for everything they do. If a sanguine is married to a phlegmatic or choleric, they seldom receive much approval. Only melancholies seem to voice an understanding word of approval. This is only because they understand the emotional hurt the sanguine feels. While I'm at it, take the word "but" out of your vocabulary when speaking to a sanguine. Whenever anyone says to a sanguine; "You did a nice job making your bed this morning, but…" Or, "You look OK today, but…" you do nothing but crush their spirit. Phrases, sentences or expressions with the word "but" following (a favorite expression with melancholies) have never helped a sanguine to do better next time. It only discourages them to even try. If you are married to or have sanguine children, praise them in everything they do (whether you feel like it or not) and you will see them giving more of themselves. I can guarantee it! Try it, and watch your sanguine spouse or child improve in everything they do. Praising, not scolding, works with sanguines!

To give you an example, I had been talking about writing a book with the title *Down to Earth Witnessing* for many years before I ever started on it. I didn't really have a clue what it would be about. I just liked the title. I came up with the title because I had been told over and over that I was so down to earth in the way I witnessed to others. People knew I loved them, for who they were not for what I wanted them to be, which is easy for sanguines to do. During my ordination review, a question was addressed to Kathy concerning me. She answered by saying, "David has been talking about writing a book called *Down to Earth Witnessing* for many years and that pretty well explains the way he approaches others." I was studying for my Masters at that time and had already discovered the temperament theory and was pondering the idea of that being the subject of the book. That had been as far as I had gotten. After Kathy gave me that praise however, I went home and with God's blessings, wrote my first book. (Review and Herald changed the titled to *Power Witnessing*). Praise with a sanguine will get you what you want from them. I promise it!

Sanguines also have the problem of being late for appointments. If church starts at 9:30 AM, you can almost bank on them being tardy. One time shortly after a seminar on temperaments, I had a gentleman come ask to speak to me privately about a situation he was trying to deal with. It seemed he was married to a woman who was never on time for anything. Before they were married, (it was a second marriage for both of them) her children and close acquaintances tried to warn him she is always late for everything no matter what. He had not listened. It didn't matter if she was the Sabbath School Superintendent for that day, in charge of the social, hair or doctor's appointment, or whatever, she would not be on time. Many of her church members, friends, and children had come to accept this unfortunate bad habit, but he had not. After we talked for a while, I came to the conclusion she was a sanguine for sure. I told him the only thing he could do was to accept her the way she is like the others had. She was in her 60's and changing her inconsiderate tardiness was out of the question. It would not happen without a miracle from God. I gave him some suggestions of things he could try to make his life more bearable, but his wife is who she is and no amount of reprimanding would change her. She would be late for her own funeral, and he had to face that fact.

Not only are sanguines late, they often appear to others as weak-willed, undisciplined children no matter what age they are. Sanguines don't want to grow up. They enjoy acting and playing like children. It's the sanguine grown-up outside playing with the kids more than any other temperament. They also have many, many toys and want more! I think many television commercials advertising toys are designed with children and adult sanguines in mind. (Do you have any idea how hard it is for me to write some of the things you are reading about us sanguines? But I wanted you to read it like it is. Besides, I'm praying you'll be able to handle it more easily when I start writing about your temperament. Remember that I am being truthful, no matter hard it is, about us sanguines. So when the truth is told about you... well, just be prepared.)

Chapter 4

Sanguines are prone to be spontaneous to almost anything a person says, good or bad! They love stories, especially if they're in the story. They're famous for unlimited and unrestricted amusing stories about themselves. They almost never save money and usually have the brightest clothes in the room. They are the super extroverts who thrive to be the center of attention no matter what. (Have I already said that?) Anyway, because of their sensitive, enthusiastic, talkative and bubbly spirit, I have found some spouses have excused their mate's weaknesses by saying, "Oh well, that's just the way they are."

Two areas that sanguines are weakest in are food and sexual desires. They like to eat and have very weak will power when it comes to saying "no" to food. They have the tendency to eat too fast and way too much that causes many to be overweight. They also have wandering eyes that enjoy looking at the forbidding zones of the opposite sex. Their sexual desire is almost an impossible passion that doesn't ever seem to go away. They think more about sex than any of the three other temperaments, especially sanguine men! They're more out to prove they still can, as they get older in life. But not to worry. The born again experience is real for sanguines too! God will help any sanguine control lustful passion if they will allow Him to.

A good verse to help understand a sanguine is found in Deuteronomy 6:8,9. "Do whatever you need to do so as not to forget what the Lord has said, even if you have to write it on the back of your hands or on your forehead. Write them on the doors of your houses and on your fence posts and gates" (*The Clear Word*). If there is any good habit my wife has taught me above another, it is the one of making myself notes to help me remember. You will find notes in my office, car, briefcase, and yes, on the back of my hands.

There you have it. I have let my mask down (somewhat) and let you see us sanguines for what we really feel inside. Not all of us act just like you read. Always remember that each of us has a little of the four basic temperaments and many times one of our other temperaments kick in and override our predominate temperament. For example because of my phlegmatic secondary temperament, I'm almost never late for an appointment. I'm always earlier than I have to be. So as you read through this publication, bear in mind not everyone will be exactly like I write. Keep in store that the born again experience is for real. God can change our weaknesses into strengths if we will allow Him to. We just have to be willing.

"So we have nothing in ourselves of which to boast. We have no ground for self-exaltation. Our only ground of hope is in the righteousness of Christ imputed to us, and in that wrought by His Spirit working in and through us."[2]

With the description you just read of what a sanguine is really like, is it any wonder why I titled this chapter, *"Lord Have Mercy, I Married a Motor-Mouth Joker."*

Chapter 5

"Help! I Married an Egotistical and Domineering Workaholic: *The Choleric*"

"When Christ is formed within, the hope of glory, then the truth of God will so act upon the natural temperament that its transforming power will be seen in changed characters."[1]

Years ago I was a member of a local *Radio Emergency Action Citizen Team* (REACT) organization. Each member was required to have a CB radio and respond to any emergencies they were called to. Inside that club was a gentleman with the CB handle of "Never Sweat." (A person's Handle is their CB name in case you don't understand CB lingo.) That man really lived up to his handle. I never once saw that man perspire. I don't care how hot (and it gets hot in Texas) or how hard he worked, sweat never emitted from his body. Usually most CB'ers take on a handle (name) that best fits their personality. For example, my CB handle was "Boogieman." (I liked to boogie in the 70's but that's another story). I had a good friend with the handle "Tumbling Tumbleweed." He had red hair and wore it in a huge afro that made him look like bleeding tumbling tumbleweed. "Honky Tonk" was another good friend who unfortunately lived up to his CB handle, too. And many others that I will spare you the pleasure of knowing who took on a CB handle that best describes their personality.

Do you recall any Bible characters that were named for their personality? I think of Jacob whose name meant "*supplanter* or *deceiver*." Later his name was changed to Israel which meant "*God strives or Prince with God.*" Both times he lived up to his name. How about David whose name means "*the beloved*?" Or Paul that meant "*little?*" On and on the Bible is full of people who had names that were chosen for them and who lived up to their described character.

How about you? If God were to give you a new name that would best describe your personality or character, what would it be? If a name that characterized you the best were placed in a book or on your tombstone, what would you want it to be? It's something to think about. Maybe in the 70's I would have liked "Boogieman" placed on my tombstone, but not today!

Can you keep from sweating on a hot summer day? Not unless you can find a cool spot or you are like my friend "Never Sweat." I'm one of the unfortunate ones who sweat constantly. No matter how much I want to stop sweating, I can't unless I get in front of a fan or find a cool breeze. And even then, there's no guarantee that my pores will close shut. Near most of the pulpits I speak from, you will find a fan. Sweating profoundly is just a part of my genetic chromosome combination that I was born with. I guess my CB handle could have been "Always Sweat" if I wanted to describe one of my natural body functions.

Again, please allow me to emphasize the reality that neither you nor I can help how our emotions feel naturally. What we feel inside comes as involuntarily as my sweating does. There is not a thing in the world we can do about it. But we can learn, with God's help, how to react to our natural emotions.

If you should ask anyone why he or she acts the way they do, most would say, "Because I feel like doing it," or "It feels good doing it." But why do we feel like doing certain things and why does it feel good doing it? How about the Christian who does things they do not want to do, but does it anyway. Paul said in Romans 7:15–24 RSV: "I do not understand my own actions. For I do not do what I want, but I do the very thing I hate... So then it is no longer I that do it, but sin which dwells within me, that is, in my flesh. I can will what is right, but I cannot do it... Wretched man that I am! Who will deliver me from this body of death?"

Temperaments can be both easy to understand and at the same time difficult to understand. Every time I think I'm about to break the code of understanding an individual temperament, along comes something new which throws almost everything I had researched out the door. I find myself having to start the investigation all over again.

It's easier for me to understand the sanguine/phlegmatic man and why they do what they do. I know where they are coming from and why. But it is very difficult for me to understand why cholerics, melancholies or women do what they do. I have never, nor will I ever, walk in a choleric's, melancholy's or woman's shoes. Let me give you some illustrations. If I asked a melancholy why everything has to be perfect and in order, he or she would simply say, "Because it feels right." They reason, why do any task half way? It must be done precisely and accurately or don't do it at all. (A weakness of a sanguine). Or if I asked a choleric what is the urgency that he or she be the leader, they would simply explain that they're the best one for the job. Cholerics sense the feeling that it would be the right and best thing to place them in full supervision of any undertaking. This natural born leader would feel it is their assigned responsibility to take over any project so that it would be done right the first time.

If you should ask one of us sanguines why we enjoy having fun all the time; why we need everything to be fun and exciting every waking moment; why do we act like children; our answer would be simple, it feels good and brings us enjoyment! We delight in being sociable and joking with others. Ask a phlegmatic why he doesn't get excited or why he avoids conflicts? Ask how they can stay so peaceful during a crisis. He or she would plainly state that taking life slow and easy is more relaxing and keeping a cool head in the midst of a crisis will help you live longer.

The bottom line is this. Everything a person does feels right to them personally. It may not make sense to someone else, but to that individual with his unique temperament combination, it is simply the right thing to do. Remember, no two people think, act, behave, or respond the same way.

The next key issue I want you to understand is your own temperament in the light in which God sees it. In other words, how does the Lord see us when things we do come naturally? It's sad but true, most of us, when we're doing wrong, think we're doing right.

I thought I was doing the right thing the time I gave a puppet show where my dodo bird, Clyde, laid an egg. To many others, and me the skit was cute and funny, but it offended two ladies. They thought I was making fun of a woman's childbirth. Since then I have found a few other women who felt uncomfortable with the skit but never said anything to me. Here was something that felt right, funny and pleasurable to me, but distasteful to a few others.

This makes me wonder. How does God see the things we do that seem so right and feels so good? Do we often behave or respond to different situations in a way that grieves the heart of God? Of course we do. I believe that most everything we do or say would turn out in a more positive way if we would only stop and think before we spoke or acted. (One of the sanguine's and choleric's strongest weakness is they speak or act before they think. Ouch!) Each of us must learn to practice self-discipline, to think before we speak. This is especially important when speaking to our own family members. I don't know why it is that we have this tendency to hurt and disappoint the ones we love. We will speak and behave in such a way with our own family members that we would never even consider doing in front of others. "Self-denial must be practiced in the home. Every member of the family should be kind and courteous, and should studiously seek by every word and act to bring in peace, contentment, and happiness. *All members of the family do not have the same disposition, the same stamp of character*; but through self-discipline, and love and forbearance one for another, all can be bound together in the closest union. In many families there is not that Christian politeness, that true courtesy, deference, and respect for one another that would prepare its members to marry and make happy families of their own. In the place of patience, kindness, tender courtesy, and Christian sympathy and love, there are sharp words, clashing ideas, and a criticizing, dictatorial spirit. In every family where Christ abides, a tender interest and love will be manifested for one another; not a spasmodic love expressed only in fond caresses, but a love that is deep and abiding. True love is a high and holy principle, and is altogether different in character from that love that is awakened by impulse, and which suddenly dies when tested and tried."[2]

As you read the next few chapters, please keep in mind I picked on my temperament first. I opened up and told it like it is. I "let my hair down," kicked off my shoes and removed (partly) my mask. I explained in the simplest language that I knew, both the good as well as the bad about us sanguines. You sanguines reading this book probably hate me by now! Sorry. But I had to tell our inner secrets so that I might be able to bring out the weaknesses as well as the strengths of the other temperaments without them hating me more than they do.

So let's start with the next temperament, the temperament my oldest son, David Jr. has. The natural, born-to-lead leader, the choleric. The choleric is the little boy or girl who is forced to sit in a chair but soon remarks, "My body may be sitting down, but inside I'm standing up."

David Jr. is the stand up "I'm in charge" family member who has been ever since he was an infant. He knew what he wanted out of life at an early age, and he knew how to get it. Believe it or not, (and I have a picture to prove it is true) when he was only six months old he was reaching for his spoon to feed himself. He didn't want us to feed him. Older in life he would stand his ground and not budge an inch. It didn't matter what sort of punishment I'd administer, he would not move one iota from what he had his mind set on. (Sad to say, he hasn't changed much since becoming an adult).

A Powerful Marriage

David Jr. is one of the most stubborn persons I know. (Sorry son, but it is true). He has been since he was old enough to walk and talk. (Have you ever noticed how we parents spend the first seven or eight years of our child's life helping them to walk and talk? Then the next ten years to sit down and shut up!) As a child he was going to have his way no matter what. His strong choleric nature would stand up, speak up and take charge every time. He would demand his way. A phlegmatic can be headstrong too. They also at times dig their heels in and will not give an inch. If a phlegmatic believes he is right, then don't push him into a corner, because he will come out swinging. Since my secondary temperament is phlegmatic, several times Jr. and I would have our moments.

As I have already pointed out, I find it very difficult understanding why others do what they do. But there have been many (my wife would say a few) times in my own life when I have done something that I can't explain why I did it. All of us have to be ready for the Holy Spirit to guide us. He may lead us into doing something that we can't explain later, something that is totally out of character for us. That happened to me on a hot summer day in west Texas.

Neither David Jr. nor I will ever forget the time when we were on our way over to visit my friend, Gary Moore, in west Texas. Junior was about ten years old. Before we arrived he had disobeyed me, so I patiently informed him he was going to get a paddling when we reached our destination. We were still about fifteen minutes away, so I hoped this would give him enough time to ponder the fact that he was about to receive a spanking and why. But instead of it worrying him, it only made him that much more angry. When we arrived I told him to follow me to the backyard, which he did. But before I knew what had happened, he had picked up a water hose and commenced to show me who was going to receive the correction. For some reason, and to this day I still don't know why, I did nothing but stand there and let my ten-year old hit me.

Chapter 5

He continued to whack me with that hose for what seemed forever. Yes, he left marks on me. (Father abuse maybe?) I did nothing but stand there and look straight into his eyes with every swing he took. Finally he stopped, and I had never nor since then seen him cry like he did at that moment. There was just something about not doing anything that broke his little stubborn choleric heart. To this day he often recalls that moment. He says, "Dad, there was nothing you could have done that would have hurt me more than you standing there and doing nothing." He could see the hurt in my face, and it touched him in a way he had never been touched before. Did this stop him and me from ever having tense moments throughout his teen years? No, but he never again picked up something to hit me with.

We have to accept the fact that just because people act differently, doesn't make them wrong. Was I wrong to stand there and allow my son to hit me? Any answer you give will be correct, because the outcome served the purpose. David was punished, just not by me, he punished himself. It may have been the only way to reach his heart and God knew it. The Lord stopped me from doing what I wanted to do. (No I would not have used it on him. I would have used my belt!) All of us must be prepared for God to use us in ways we might not normally do. When we encounter the born again experience, God will work through us in ways we never dreamed we would or could do.

I often find it fun trying to understand why some individuals do what they do. I don't try to make excuses for them, but I have come to the point that often I can laugh at the different temperament traits I see in people. What is really funny is when I find out that some folks think I act odd, too.

The choleric, unless he has his strengths under control, possibly has the hardest spontaneous nature to accept of the four temperaments. For some reason cholerics love to fight, both physically and mentally. They treasure demonstrating they're right by arguing with anyone over anything to prove it. No matter what, you can't win an argument with a choleric! If two cholerics get in a showdown, watch out, for

World War III is about to begin. Cholerics like to think they have their act together. But one of their down sides is they have a hard time controlling their temper, and they can become extremely hostile. They're the table pounder, horn blowing, obscene hand sign, screaming, and door slamming individual. I do know some who have learned to control their anger; however, an explosion into a violent performance is always possible with them. I've seen some cause pain in others and enjoy it. It doesn't take them long to reach the conclusion that most people wilt under their outbursts. A choleric will not hesitate to do what it takes for them to accomplish and achieve whatever they want. They will do whatever it takes to have their way. They can be bossy and domineering. They wear the pants in the family. It doesn't matter whether they're the husband or wife, it is the choleric who runs the household. In some households this can cause problems, especially if the choleric is the wife. For some reason we men just don't like being bossed around by women. I've seen cholerics curse, argue, beg, and throw items when something isn't going their way. I know one choleric man who got so upset with his wife that he picked up his expensive guitar and hurled it through their glass window. But praise the Lord, at least he didn't throw it at his wife! Unless God's Holy Spirit controls him, a choleric's temper can get him into a lot of trouble.

Cholerics are active, strong-willed, sarcastic, independent, self-sufficient, hot headed, and quick thinking. They find it very easy to make decisions for themselves and the rest of the family. They love a challenge and are full of determination to make everything work but they can be very bull-headed while doing it. Their temper is the very reason they must pray "daily" that the Holy Spirit will help them control their anger and tongue.

Like a sanguine, the choleric is an extrovert, just not as intense. He is probably the hardest worker. They never know when to stop. They're the work-a-holic of all temperaments. They thrive on staying busy. This often causes problems in their home because they don't see the need to spend time with their spouse or children.

They're the ones who usually work themselves to death. This eager beaver temperament is very common in North America and other Western nations. They're the spouse you will find who is very difficult to convince he (she) needs to slow down and take life a little easier. Cholerics consider anyone who doesn't work at least 18-hour days to be weak. Needless to say, this drives the spouse crazy. Because of this work pattern, many marriage partners go looking elsewhere for love and companionship. The choleric has a hard time understanding why his or her spouse doesn't appreciate them for trying to make a good living and life easier for them. This doesn't have to take place at their employment either. It can be yard work, church work, sports, housework, etc. Cholerics become obsessed with competing in as many activities as possible. Even going on a vacation with the family can become exhausting because the choleric wants to see and do as much as possible before the day is up.

I recall the Sabbath morning when we were to vote into fellowship a woman by the name of Aline DuBose. She had requested her membership to be transferred from another church. Trying to pronounce her last name correctly I asked if her name was pronounced Da-Boss? A huge laugh was heard throughout the church as many expressed, "That's Aline, da-boss!"

Cholerics have great self-control, but they have a hard time understanding why their spouse and children don't possess the same will power they have. David Jr. cannot understand why I don't want to buy into money marketing like he has. He is sold with the idea that in forty or so years he will be a millionaire. He is learning to save money, which I think is great, because we sanguines have a hard time saving a penny. But now he considers it to be every person's duty to save money just as he is. So he is on a one-man crusade to convince the world to buy into money marketing. Good-luck son!

Cholerics have the strange ability to look at others with an expression that will melt an iceberg. Unfortunately they let their self-examining behavior get in their way of understanding the temperaments of others.

Since cholerics must have everything their own way and don't always get it, they become unhappy and will not mind telling you so. This is especially true when it comes to their spouse and children. They demand respect. Cholerics learn young in life that if they scream long and loud enough, others will give into their demands. This was the biggest problem I had with David Jr. He wanted to stay and live with my folks every time we went for a visit. He would throw such fits that after a while my folks and I would give in and let him stay. Now years later we know this wasn't the best thing to do. I wish I had known then what I know now because my response would have been different.

I've found a few (very few) cholerics who will try guilt manipulation, whining, or nagging instead of pounding a table to have their way. Years ago I ministered to a choleric woman who would whine and nag me for what seemed hours to get me to do what she wanted done. She very seldom showed her temper, but I could see it in her eyes. Usually I didn't have the time to do what she asked of me, but I gave in just to shut her nagging and whining up. She knew how to manipulate me into submission: another weakness of us sanguines.

If there is any one temperament above another that believes an individual can cease instantly any bad habit or sinning altogether, that instant victory is possible, it's the choleric. Anyone who makes this claim doesn't fully comprehend the other temperaments. While the statement is true, nevertheless, it is very difficult for melancholies and sometimes sanguines to accept the fact that God loves them enough to forgive them and give them instant victory. Cholerics have the hardest time understanding why others cannot just throw away their cigarettes, liquor, porno magazines, etc., like they did. They feel that if they could do it, then so can everyone else. Because of their powerful self-discipline trait they have no idea how intense the battle is for others to fight. They fully believe everyone should have the strength they have, and if they don't, then they perceive their faith as weak.

If there is one character trait above another that I admire about David Jr., it is his ability that once his mind is made up to do something, he does it and nothing will stop him. I've watched him quit smoking cold turkey. I've seen him drop two hundred pounds (yes, you read correctly) in less than a year and I've witnessed him as he built his sewing machine business into a thriving enterprise when times were tough. All this and more because of his strong will power—a characteristic the melancholies and sanguines are weak in.

On the flip side, I also personally know some choleric Christians who are the first to boast they haven't sinned for days, weeks, months, and yes, even years. I'll never forget the day during a church function when I asked the question, "Is there anyone here who has gone through the entire day and hasn't sinned yet?" And you guessed it. The one strong choleric present that evening immediately raised her hand and replied that she had not. Then she proceeded to glance around the room at the rest of us "transgressors" and gave us the "shame on you sinners" stare that only a choleric can give.

Of the four basic temperaments, it was the choleric God created to be the natural leader. Because of their self-discipline and overflowing self-determination, they can persuade others to follow them. They will finish what they start. You will see him or her the happiest (that is if they are in charge) when they are working on some worthwhile project. They don't need to stop to analyze a project or situation like a melancholy does, they just do it and review their work later. Then if others don't like how the project turned out, well that's just too bad, because the choleric doesn't care what others think about his and her performance. They are going to do it their way regardless. You'd better just get out of their way.

A good verse for the choleric to learn is John 3:3 NIV, "I tell you the truth, no one can see the kingdom of God unless he is born again." I believe Paul was no doubt a choleric. At one time he was the sort of leader who would have eliminated every man, woman, and child who called themselves a Christian. But then one day on a dusty road headed toward Damascus, God called him to become one of the greatest leaders of all humanity (Acts 9:1–9). Paul once wrote that he had to "die daily" (1 Corinthians 15:31) because he was the "chief among sinners" (1 Timothy 1:15). Paul's conversion is proof positive that the born again experience is real. Saul, the hotheaded, proud, arrogant, domineering and persecuting leader becomes Paul the born-again, Spirit filled, and dynamic, independent, self-disciplined servant leader. If you're a choleric, with help from the Holy Spirit, you too can be transformed just like Paul was. Your hard, angry, impetuous, self-sufficient traits can be replaced with a gentle, considerate, concerned, and sociable quality that others will cherish. You can become the father, mother, husband or wife God would be proud to call His son or daughter. Pray daily that the Holy Spirit will guide you into knowing how to control your temper and tongue. His promise is, "Therefore if any man (or woman) be in Christ, he (or she) is a new creature: old things are passed away; behold, all things are become new" 2 Corinthians 5:17.

After reading this chapter, do you still feel pity for the spouses of sanguines and cholerics? Well don't feel too disheartened yet until after you have read about the sensitive, creative, analytical, orderly, faithful, perfectionist, suspicious, melancholy marriage partner.

Chapter 6

"The Six Million-Dollar Man and the Bionic Woman: *The Melancholy*"

"Many who profess to be Christ's followers have an anxious, troubled heart because they are afraid to trust themselves with God. They do not make a complete surrender to Him, for they shrink from the consequences that such a surrender may involve. Unless they do make this surrender they cannot find peace." [1] "The members of the family *do not all have the same stamp of character*, and there will be frequent occasion for the exercise of patience and forbearance; but through love and self-discipline all may be bound together in the closest union. "[2]

To demonstrate this next temperament I would like to introduce you to two of the most beautiful and closest women in my life; my wife Kathy, and our daughter, Tonya. If there is any one thing I have learned about living with my two melancholy beauties it is this; they both by far have the richest and most compassionate of all temperaments. I guess mainly because melancholies are very analytical, self-sacrificing, gifted, and perfectionists.

I have often questioned over and over why God would bless me with two angels like He has. Over the past twenty plus years I have stood in the doorway of our bedroom and looked at the most precious and treasured gift a man could be blessed with. A woman who is much wiser and gifted than I am. I often think; "Lord, Kathy deserves someone much better looking than me. She's entitled to a man who administers much more patience than I can. Someone who can give her more than what I have been able to." Then I crawl into bed with the same woman who would argue that fact and tell me from the bottom of her heart that I'm the best thing God has given her. I know, for she has told me this time and time again. Not always in words, for you see melancholies often talk with their deeds. Actions speak louder than words with a melancholy. I haven't always understood that, but it's true. With careful and loving hands Kathy has often placed a sweet nothing note in my sack lunch. She has mailed me aromatic cards whenever I'm out of town for a while. She has made my favorite dessert (banana-pudding) on most of our anniversaries.

Often when she is asleep I've noticed her hair hides the beauty of her face, but the light from her countenance always shines through. As I stand there in the doorway and wonder; why in the world would God entrust a stumbling, awkward old fool like me with the task of loving and leading such a treasure. I think, remarkable Lord, I get to spend my entire life with her.

Kathy is a very light sleeper. I know I would wake her if I touched her, so instead of leaning over to kiss her, I often kiss my hand and blow it her way. Thank You Lord. If only every man was as blessed as me.

As I type this section of the book, I can't help but remember how Kathy and I started dating. As I mentioned in chapter one, Kathy and I worked for the same man who owned two restaurants that were beside each other. She was a waitress at a Pizza Inn and I worked next door at Taco Rio. I had recently gone through a bad divorce several months earlier and was about to go on my first real date. My ex-wife had left me for a sixteen-year-old, and I had a hard time dealing with that. Time has its way of healing broken hearts. So I asked a young woman I had met at work out for a date. Let me pause for a moment and give you a little background about myself. I had been raised a Seventh-day Adventist, but at this time in my life I had walked away from almost everything I had been taught. I was a drug addict and had been known to sell drugs. I drank very heavily, smoked, and ran around with wild women. My hair was long, and I dressed in loud and colorful clothes (remember now, I'm a sanguine).

Chapter 6

My language was also very colorful which I didn't try hiding.

On this so-called date, I had the drugs and beer back at my apartment where I planned to take this young woman. We were to meet at Pizza Inn at 8:00 that evening. To make a long story short, she never made it. I had been stood up. My first date after going through a divorce, and there I sat at the table, 8:30 pm, looking sad and depressed. Kathy had been talking to me off and on that evening and somehow looking at my puppy dog eyes, she could tell I was really blue. I had told her I was to meet my date at 8:00 and she knew by now I had been stood up. Her compassionate side of her temperament kicked in and she walked over and said she was getting off at 9:00 and wondered if I would like to come to her apartment and have cookies and Kool-Aid with her and her six-year-old daughter.

You talk about a switch! From drugs and beer to cookies and Kool-Aid. From my bachelor's pad to her nicely arranged apartment. From a wild date to a sweet and innocent woman. To this day I still do not know what impressed Kathy to ask me over. Knowing Kathy the way I do today, I was anything but her dreamboat of a date. You will never convince me there isn't a God who works miracles and impresses people to do things they would never normally do. No innocent Seventh-day Adventist woman (melancholy on top of that) would ever invite someone like me over to her apartment for an evening. God, however, does work in mysterious ways.

I realized later that if someone at Pizza Inn had overheard I was being invited to Kathy's apartment, would have wondered if she had lost her mind. I'm sure we became the butt of their jokes that evening. I still wonder what any of the saints at church would have thought if they had seen me walking up with Kathy to her apartment that night. Knowing what I know today about melancholies, it still puzzles me. You see melancholies are very concerned with what people think about them. They, and so does the

A Powerful Marriage

sanguine, have a hard time handling it if people think badly of them.

Most people would have considered me to be a very unlikely candidate for a church visit. Most would have saved their seed sowing for better soil. They might have been right except Jesus had another plan for Kathy and I, a plan for our life together that we would have never guessed in a million years. I can't thank Him enough for the two melancholies in my world today. I also thank Kathy for listening to Him when He impressed her to do something she probably would never have done in ten million years. Even with her strong compassionate side, melancholies still have their high standards, and I was far from being the perfect date. I want to thank her for caring not only then, but today as well. Thank you Kathy for the examples of what being a Christian is all about. Thanks for taking the courage to offer me some of the Bread of Life you held that evening so many years ago. I love you.

Well, excuse me for a minute while I grab a box of Kleenex. Sometimes reminiscing about the advantages of being married to the most wonderful wife in the world chokes me up.

One of the beauties of a melancholy is that they would argue the fact they are the most wonderful. They are the most humble of all temperaments. In fact, it would really surprise me if my wife doesn't ask me to leave this story out. If it's still there, however, it would be one debate I won. She is so humble, too humble for us sanguines who want the whole world to know how blessed and wonderful we are.

Since melancholies are the people who are so humble, they seldom want their name mentioned. They are the behind-the-scene type person. Kathy often makes me look like a great pastor. People rarely see what she's done that looks as if I did it. She will send a card to a sick or missing member with my name signed at the bottom. I constantly have members thanking me for the sweet and thoughtful card they received that week. It's in Kathy's nature that I look good. She sacrificed her career as a teacher to help me full time in the ministry. She does many of those nuts and bolts jobs, which make me look like a professional pastor. It often pains her to see me do something dumb and foolish. (You're right; I keep her in a lot of pain). You see melancholies must have everything perfect, even his or her spouse. So they will do things to make their spouse look good. The downside is no one is perfect. Melancholies have an impossible time accepting this fact.

Because melancholies need everything to be perfect, they often find it hard understanding why anyone would even mull with the idea of ever doing a job halfway. Probably one of their most difficult hurdles is they don't mind explaining to others when their act isn't together. This can make other temperaments very agitated. It's not that I get upset when Kathy tells me to do something; I get upset when she wants me to do it *her* way.

We have a cellular phone that I like to charge on a small glass table next to the front door. I leave it there so I can remember it when I leave. Recently we had company coming over who was going to be staying with us for a few days. By this time Kathy was tired of having the phone charger always sitting where it was the first thing people saw when they enter our home. So she called me into the living room and proceeded to tell me where we were going to be keeping the charger from now on. I started laughing. At one time it would've really upset me to have her tell me what "we" were going to do. There wasn't any asking where I would like to keep it; it was "we" are going to keep it behind the television where no one could see it. Because of understanding her melancholy/choleric temperament, I just stood there laughing. She was puzzled at what I thought was so funny about moving a charger.

While observing other melancholies I have found many have the cleanest, neatest homes, and cars. Their lawns look picture perfect. Every leaf and blade of grass lays the same way. They will trim and trim until every blade is the exact same height. Tonya and her husband recently bought a new home and the first time I visited, I was in for a shock! It was clean and very tidy. It could stand the white glove test and pass. I remembered her room while she was at home as a child. It always looked like a tornado had hit it. She worried me with the thought of what her home would look like when she grew up. I'm glad to see her temperament finally took control of her teenage lifestyle.

Melancholies also have a very sensitive emotional nature and like the sanguine, can be hurt at the drop of a pin. They receive more enjoyment from the finer arts than the rest of the temperaments. They are introverts who give way to different moods. They can be lifted to the seventh heaven one moment and found depressed and despondent the next.

Melancholies are probably the best caretakers and feel responsible for people more than any other temperament. They will easily drop whatever they're doing to help someone else. This can cause problems in some marriages because people outside their marriage are receiving more attention than those inside.

Another strength of a melancholy is they have a logical and analytical mind that can explain almost anything better than the rest. They have great memory and concentration skills. At home Tonya could watch television and have the radio playing while at the same time doing her homework and still make straight A's. However, at the same time, because they diagnose and analyze everything in such detail, they can have some irrational and illogical beliefs. Since they perceive in their mind that everything and everybody must be perfect, the melancholy is often found depressed. Tonya and Kathy both become very depressed if they do not feel they have done their best. I have discovered almost every person who comes to me for counseling is a melancholy. I don't mean that in a negative way. Its just melancholies have the hardest time dealing with imperfection.

Kathy likes to plan everything out on a time scheduled. Almost daily she comes into my office and compares her schedule with mine. All is fine until something upsets her agenda, then she is depressed the rest of the day.

Chapter 6

I'll never forget the day (although I wish I could) when we were about to go out of town and Kathy had a list of things on her agenda she wanted to finish before we left. My sanguine temperament was in its usual hurry to get on the road. Before our agreed set time had arrived I walked into her office and asked if she was ready to go. She said yes, grabbed her purse, and headed for the van. Without knowing that I had upset her I felt great; we were going to get away early. But before we were out of the driveway I knew something was wrong. (Husband intuition I guess). She wasn't talking. When a melancholy is upset they are very quite. I asked what was wrong, and the moment she said, "Nothing" I knew something had happened. After a couple minutes of asking her to please tell me what was wrong, she finally did. She had been writing out checks to pay this month's bills before we left. It was the last thing on her list to finish before we left. The day before we had agreed we would leave at a certain time, and she was keeping within that time schedule. I had tried bumping the time up, and this didn't set well with her. Melancholies have a dire need to finish what they start, and they do not like it when their schedule is bumped. So after realizing what I had done, I said I was sorry and turned around and returned home so we would still have the electricity on when we returned from our trip.

Melancholies have a hard time accepting the mistakes of themselves or others. I once had a melancholy tell me that if he finds one mistake in a book or magazine he is reading, he will put the book down and not finish it because he has lost faith in the author and editor. Because of their inclination to always be perfect in everything they do along with having everyone else refined, they are often discouraged and disappointed. Let me repeat something I wrote in *Power Witnessing*, about melancholies. "They are the chief among those to gratify. They have what some like to call the four "isms" that's hard for the other three temperaments to take. They have skepticism, pessimism, cynicism, and criticism."

I think Ellen White had melancholies in mind when she wrote; "We are in a world of suffering. Difficulty, trial, and sorrow await us all along the way to the heavenly home. But there are many who make life's burdens doubly heavy by continually anticipating trouble. If they meet with adversity or disappointment they think that everything is going to ruin, that theirs is the hardest lot of all that they are surely coming to want. Thus they bring wretchedness upon themselves and cast a shadow upon all around them. Life itself becomes a burden to them. But it need not be thus. It will cost a determined effort to change the current of their thought. But the change can be made. Their happiness, both for this life and for the life to come, depends upon their fixing their minds upon cheerful things. Let them look away from the dark picture, which is imaginary, to the benefits which God has strewn in their pathway, and beyond these to the unseen and eternal."[3]

While the choleric is hard to please, the melancholy is impossible to satisfy. They have a hard time trusting anyone, including God. I've had many of them tell me they do not want anyone controlling their life. Some melancholies have informed me they want God to take control of their life, but yet at the same time they feel afraid to let go. They hate being hurt or disappointed as much as they hate disappointing or hurting someone else. They feel they have let God down so much that He could never love and forgive them. So their trust of anyone wavers in the wind.

I don't think we can begin to understand how this must make God feel. It has to hurt Him when He offers His children so much to make them happy; and then some back away fearfully, thinking that He wants to harm or cut away what little joy they have.

Through counseling I have found many melancholies see God as an angry dictator needing to be appeased. When this happens I like to show them what 1 John 4:7,8,16 says: "Beloved, let us love one another: for love is of God; and every one that loveth is born of God, and knoweth God. He that loveth not knoweth not God; for God is love. And we

Chapter 6

have known and believed the love that God hath to us. God is love; and he that dwelleth in love dwelleth in God, and God in him." These texts imply that there never has been nor ever will be a time when God is not love. God does everything possible to lead everyone to understand that He loves us, that He is good, and that He cares what happens to us.

Kathy's melancholy temperament often embarrasses me whenever we go on trips. She has the habit of taking enough clothes and shoes for a month even if we are only going to be gone for a couple of days. One time she was headed for a Women's Retreat in our eight-passenger van. Five other ladies were to ride with her. After I carried her baggage to our van, I soon discovered her shoeboxes alone took up almost half of the luggage space! I still have no idea where the other ladies placed their things. Kathy wants to have all of the comforts of home with her whenever she travels (I don't know if that is temperament or a woman thing). Because you never know what the weather will be like in the south, she likes having a different suit of clothes just in case it turns cold or warm. She never wants to be seen in the same outfit twice. This would not be so bad except she wants a pair of shoes to match each outfit! I get so embarrassed every time I start unloading the van whenever we go to visit friends. They must think we are moving in with them.

I've discovered it's often hard to see ourselves the way others see us. We have a hard time seeing beyond our own nose. I feel we need to learn how to look in self-mirrors more regularly. I used to wonder if I really ever embarrassed Kathy until one day the truth came out.

Some years back we were called to pastor a new district. As always we started off meeting the members as soon as possible. One young lady that had quit coming to church some time earlier was on my list to visit as soon as possible. The day came and after only visiting with her for a few minutes I soon realized she was a bona fide, full fledged sanguine if I've ever-met one. She was even more sanguine than I am! And that's a lot of sanguine! She walks with a fast bounce, always eager to see what someone else is doing. She is constantly smiling and happy to meet anyone. This lady was enthusiastic beyond belief just to be involved in anything, especially if it's going to be fun.

Right off we established a friendship. She had a horse and offered to let me ride him on several occasions. We had many of the same likes and dislikes. She was into computers, reading good books, camping, and having all sorts of fun. She loved it when after asking me a Bible question I had to pull out my laptop to find the answer. She said; "Now ain't that clever. A computer that has the Bible in it." Soon she and her daughter requested for baptism.

They started attending church again along with her young son. Before long she invited her boy friend (who I had the honor of marrying to her later). Her face would sparkle and brighten up the Sanctuary every Sabbath as she entered through the church doors. Without wasting anytime she accepted different positions helping in various Sabbath School departments. From her actions, everyone knew she was a sanguine, but from her speech and accent it was also obvious she was a genuine, authentic, unquestionable countryfide rural woman. One thing about Teri; she always had a good attitude about everything.

Shortly after her first Sabbath back, Teri wanted to respond to everything said in Sabbath School. Obviously she was having fun participating in the class. She likes to chit chat with everyone after church. Some of the new members must have thought she was a little uncanny by the looks in their eyes. Teri will ask questions but answer her own inquiry before anyone would have time to respond. She derives joy from anyone who will listen to her.

We all shared and enjoyed her special moment at her wedding reception. As her new husband and she were opening their gifts, she often would let out a squeal; you would have thought she was calling the pigs for dinner. She would yell, "Mike, look at this! Ain't it prrretty?" Or "Look, someone gave us towwels." (She has that southern drawl that likes to add syllables to certain words). She giggled at some of the gifts and looked perplexed at the ones she didn't quite know what they were. She never missed a thing.

Teri is always a delight to be around. But like so many of us sanguines, she often talks loudly and so much that she can get on your nerves. I'll never forget the time when I asked Kathy if I'm anything like Teri, and quickly she replied; "All the time!" I could have crawled under a rock.

Yes, it's hard to see ourselves the way others see us. We don't always like what we see when we meet someone who acts just like we do. We have a hard time admitting we are like we are. Yet every one of us has his or her flaws. The melancholy probably has the hardest time accepting this.

In the chapter "Mask or Not to Mask?" I will explore more into the world of melancholies. Until then, do you feel sorry for the spouse's of cholerics, melancholies, and sanguines? Well don't feel too bad because we still have the peaceful and slow moving phlegmatic to look at.

Chapter 7

"The Tenacious Peacemaker: *The Phlegmatic*"

It's time now to introduce Kathy's and my baby, Charles Newkirk Farmer, whom I nicknamed Kirk, shortly after he was born. He's the easy going tenacious phlegmatic of the family, although I recently discovered he scored high as a melancholy too. Which makes him a super, super introvert. One that is peaceful, kindhearted, sensitive, creative, analytical, schedule-oriented, orderly, faithful, perfectionist, self-sacrificing, suspicious, unenthusiastic, shy, indecisive, stubborn, indifferent, lazy, and compromises too much.

Each of the adjectives above describes my son to the letter. He proved my theory right that if I ever guess someone's temperament before I test him or her and discover that I am wrong, they almost always have been a melancholy. It's not uncommon for a melancholy to appear as another temperament. As we'll see in the chapter about wearing masks, a melancholy doesn't want you to see their real feelings. Many hide behind a disguise of smiles and joy. Kirk and I both scored very high as a phlegmatic. It's this side of his temperament he allows others to meet the most. He hides many of his deep emotional feelings. In fact I was shocked at what I really learned about Kirk's temperament. But this explained many questions I had about him. For example. Why is his apartment always so clean in the living room and kitchen, but his bedroom looks like a war zone? Why are the clothes he wears always perfectly ironed and clean yet he never picks his garments up off the floor? They lay in the same spot he threw them until he has run out of something to wear and has to wash them. Why does he have to nit-pick and be so critical of everyone else's lifestyle? Now

Chapter 7

I understand why he is so stingy and stubborn. I used to think, "surely Lord, someone switched babies on me at the hospital when he was born." He is nothing like the rest of the Farmer family.

I remember the first time Kirk rode in my little '95 Toyota Tercel. He did nothing but complain about how small it was. I should have bought a four door. Why didn't I get one with cruise control? It's the ugliest green he had ever seen. Over and over he found things he didn't like. It wasn't until he realized he had hurt my feelings before he said he was sorry. This is the way introverts act. They don't mind at all criticizing something, but when they realize they have hurt someone's feelings, they soon feel bad they said anything and apologize. Where the choleric might say it but not mean it, when the phlegmatic or melancholy apologizes, they usually are truly sorry. But their apology soon wears off because in a few minutes they find something else to criticize.

One positive side of Kirk is he can keep a cool head in any crises. I recall the time when he called me on the phone and said, "Daddy, you're going to kill me!" I said, "What son, what happened?" He had disobeyed me by riding his motorcycle on the highway and pulled out in front of a pickup and had been hit. He proceeded to inform me that I was to meet with the police in the morning. He was only thirteen, and the policeman wrote him up with not having a driver's license, failing to yield to traffic, riding a dirt bike on a public highway, no license tag, and on and on the list went. I only asked, "Son are you OK?"

When I got home that night, Kirk was worried how I might react but kept his cool and made no excuses why he had disobeyed me. I never spoke a harsh word or lost my cool either. We just looked at how badly the motorcycle had been damaged. We talked about if it could be repaired or not. The next morning he and I drove to the police station where I was not prepared for what happened. The policeman must have been a father and phlegmatic himself also. He never spoke a harsh word, even though I knew he could throw the book at me. My son apologized for driving where he had been told not to and we left. No ticket(s). No throwing the book at me. Nothing. He just told my son he was lucky he wasn't hurt when the truck hit him. On the way home I again spoke nothing to him about disobeying. He kept waiting for me to be upset; kept waiting for me to take his motorcycle away from him. I guess because of my phlegmatic temperament side and remembering how my phlegmatic father had always treated me when I had disobeyed him, I was able to stay calm and so did Kirk.

Now some ten years later, Kirk has never forgotten that moment. He admits today that experience probably taught him more about what being a loving, forgiving, Christian father is. I told him that is the way our Heavenly Father is to us when we disobey Him. God is sad and hurt when we disobey, but He loves us nevertheless. Kirk knew I was hurt, but he also knew I loved him.

Now in his early twenties, Kirk has determined to make something of himself. He recently received his GED and started college, majoring in business. He fought long and hard to get in a position where he could start back to school. Daily he laces up his Reeboks for walks in the park to keep fit and trim. Between my father, oldest son, and myself, he is the only one who doesn't have a belly hanging over his belt. He is very methodical and analytical. He wants to know how or why anything works the way it does. I recall the time at the age of nine when he asked me for an old broken down sewing machine I had thrown in my junk pile. It was good for nothing but parts. He asked that if he got it working could he have it to sell for some extra spending money. I told him he would be wasting his time but sure, he could have it. It took three days, but he finally got it sewing and sold it for twenty-five dollars. I asked him to go through the pile and find more to fix up for me to sell but no such luck. Although he is very inquisitive on how things work, at the same time he is very unenthusiastic about doing what he calls unnecessary work.

Phlegmatics are also very cautious, and they don't like taking risks. Besides being unenthusiastic they're shy, indecisive, fearful, stubborn, and probably the hardest to get motivated into doing anything. Both phlegmatics and melancholies nearly always see the negative side of everything.

Phlegmatics are the easy going, laid back people whom others perceive as lazy. It's part of their nature to take things slowly and one day at a time. Some of their good temperament traits are that they can be witty, low-key, dependable, calm, cool, and peaceful. Some have called them the natural born peacemakers. Phlegmatics are usually the most pleasant to talk to because they have nothing to say in return. They don't like to argue or disagree which makes them great spouses. They make great listeners. If they get in a disagreement with their spouse they usually can stay calm, cool, and collected. That is until you back them in a corner. They then become very stubborn. They like to think before they tackle a job. They would rather settle a disagreement than to battle it out. They have a great sense of humor. They, like the melancholy, are very dependable. They like to fulfill their obligations and are always on time for appointments. Phlegmatics are very practical, efficient, and are not inclined to make heedless and unexpected decisions. Although not as much of a perfectionist as a melancholy, they do have the capability of accuracy and precision.

I have discovered one of the phlegmatics' greatest weakness is, they hate changes. When it comes time to adding a room or moving, they won't do it without dragging their feet. They hate being hurt or disappointed. They are known as the world's natural worrywarts because they will worry about anything.

After reading about the four temperaments, you probably feel your spouse isn't that bad after all.

There you have it. A quick look at my family. Each one of us with our own temperament and style of living. I'm happy to report that now that my kids are grown, they have learned much from each other. We all picked up some of the good (in some cases the bad) of each other's temperament traits. I hope you have learned a little about temperaments in the past few chapters that have helped you understand as we continue *Learning to Live Happily Ever-After*.

Chapter 8

"There is Hope"

"Jesus wants to see happy marriages, happy firesides. The warmth of true friendship and the love that binds the hearts of husband and wife are a foretaste of heaven."[1]

I pray you didn't begin reading this book with the attitude your marriage is hopelessly irreparable and is a lost cause; that you are about to drown in a river of despondency and God doesn't really care. If this is your philosophy about your marriage, then please don't put this book down; at least not yet because I'm about to give you some hope.

David was writing to God in Psalm 139 when he said, "When I was woven together in the depths of the earth, your eyes saw my unformed body. All the days ordained for me were written in your book before one of them came to be" (15–16, NIV). God plans what each individual will be even before that soul is born into the world, but it is for the individual to decide whether he will follow this divine blueprint or not.[2] When writing about marriage one author penned; "Now, as in Christ's day, the condition of society presents a sad comment upon heaven's ideal of this sacred relation. Yet even for those who have found bitterness and disappointment where they had hoped for companionship and joy, the gospel of Christ offers a solace. The patience and gentleness which His Spirit can impart will sweeten the bitter lot. The heart in which Christ dwells will be so filled, so satisfied, with His love that it will not be consumed with longing to attract sympathy and attention to itself. And through the surrender of the soul to God, His wisdom can accomplish what human wisdom fails to do. Through the revelation of His grace, hearts that were once indifferent or estranged may be united in bonds that are firmer and more enduring than those of earth—the golden bonds of a love that will bear the test of trial."[3]

Never for one moment think God doesn't know what each of us face everyday whether it be in our marriage or in trying to survive the everyday turmoil of life. "If in our ignorance we make missteps, the Saviour does not forsake us. We need never feel that we are alone. *Angels are our companions*. The Comforter that Christ promised to send in His name abides with us. In the way that leads to the City of God there are no difficulties which those who trust in Him may not overcome. *There are no dangers which they may not escape. There is not a sorrow, not a grievance, not a human weakness, for which He has not provided a remedy*. He who took humanity upon Himself knows how to sympathize with the sufferings of humanity. Not only does Christ know every soul, and the peculiar needs and trials of that soul, but He knows all the circumstances that chafe and perplex the spirit. His hand is outstretched in pitying tenderness to every suffering child. Those who suffer most have most of His sympathy and pity. He is touched with the feeling of our infirmities, and He desires us to lay our perplexities and troubles at His feet and leave them there."[4]

I honestly feel that this chapter deserves a whole book by itself, but I have tried to cut it down and center on some key points to help you accept the fact you are not alone. There are countless millions around the globe with many of the same dilemmas you face in trying to understand his or her life partner. "None need abandon themselves to discouragement and despair. Satan may come to you with the cruel suggestion, 'Yours is a hopeless case. You are irredeemable.' *But there is hope for you in Christ*. God does not bid us overcome in our own strength. He asks us to come close to His side. Whatever difficulties we labor under, which weigh down soul and body, He waits to make us free."[5]

One of the goals I hope to reach in this book is to help married couples decipher and depict better how to discover his or her spouse's wants and needs. Also I hope to prove it is very important to understand that the needs of one are not necessarily the needs of another. I'm firmly convinced if each married person could meet the other's needs, we would have far fewer divorces than we have today. In fact, I feel, without a clear understanding of the temperament theory, a person will only be spinning their wheels on trying to meet the needs of each other. A sad fact is if one spouse cannot or will not try to meet the needs of their partner, then his or her partner cannot or will not be able to meet the other's needs. But once a person finds the key which unlocks the veil and general make-up of another, then getting along with each other becomes easier and easier with each passing day.

Let me begin by declaring the fact that any married man or woman which has taken on the assignment of trying to undergo the reasoning, motive, course of thought, and or just plain logic of why their spouse does what they do, I have some very bad news. They will fail their assignment! They will misconstrue the reasoning of their spouse almost every time. No amount of homework and research will ever give you the answers you seek. Trying to find the answer to why the opposite gender does what they do is like a minister trying to explain where God came from. It is impossible. No man alive will ever understand the true inner feelings of a woman. Her likes and dislikes, her demeanor, attitude, behavior, personality, nature, character, and general all around make up is so exactly opposite to that of a man. It is beyond a man's mentality to understand one iota of a woman's inner feelings. Even if the entire world's specialists on women teamed up and tried to explain the feelings and reasoning power of women, a man would still never comprehend a woman's true physical, mental, and rational thoughts. Nor will a woman ever be able to comprehend, grasp, and seize upon why a man behaves and conducts himself the way he does. His general all around mannerism, idiosyncrasy, and direction in life is such the opposite route of that of a woman that she is almost driven to being committed for insanity while trying to understand his reasoning.

Well, believe it or not, the exact same holds true when someone is trying to understand another person's temperament. It just cannot be done. It is next to impossible to fully understand another person's temperament that is different from yours. We can only accept the fact that temperaments, like men and women, think, comprehend, grasp, and distinguish things different than the other. It takes the same faith to believe God has always existed, as it is to accept the fact that men, women, and temperaments are different and cannot be fully understood by another. Which makes this doubly hard in marriage since we are not only trying to understand our spouse's temperament, we're also trying to understand their gender.

Through my studies and life experiences, I have found there does exist a principle for having peace and happiness in a home. A principle I believe will work for any married person who will put it into practice in their life no matter what kind of problems exist in their marriage. "The principle inculcated by the injunction, 'Be ye kindly affectioned one to another,' lies at the very foundation of domestic happiness. *Christian courtesy should reign in every household. It is cheap, but it has power to soften natures which would grow hard and rough without it.* The cultivation of a uniform courtesy, a willingness to do by others as we would like them to do by us, *would banish half the ills of life.*"[6]

As a husband and father of twenty-seven plus years, I know something of the joys and sorrows of married life. There have been and still are times when I pray asking God to overrule or reverse the bad decisions and poor influence I have made in my home. But I realize today I waste energy wallowing in remorse for my past mistakes crying out to God. "It is not wise to gather together all the unpleasant recollections of a past life, its iniquities and disappointments."[7] "We should study the experience of past life, study it just as we study the proof-sheets of an article, to find the errors and to note them on the margin of the page. We should do this daily, and note our faults so that we may avoid them in the future."[8] I wish I had spent more time noting my own faults and learning to accept and understand my family for who they are.

Oh how I wish I had received a "Farmer Family" manual when Kathy and I got married. I needed one complete with personal instruction for Kathy and each of our three children. Maybe then I could have spent more time enjoying them instead of having to apologize for my mistakes of misjudging them.

As I attempt to approach this very controversial subject on *Learning to Live Happily Ever-After* in marriage, I want you to know I do not claim to possess any secret formula or have any magic tricks up my sleeve. I have no family secrets handed down to me from my father, which had been handed down to him from his. If I had such a formula, family secret, or magic trick, I would bottle them up and make millions. Although there isn't a family secret or magic trick, I do believe there are some principles we can apply to vastly improve our marriages. Those principles are what I hope to share with you as we explore together throughout the remainder of this book.

Have you ever wondered why God planned from the very beginning that a couple of opposite temperaments were to be attracted to each other? Why would God even want opposite temperaments to attract and become one-flesh? Average couples nowadays spend most of their wedded life seemingly doing nothing more than butting heads against one another because they practically never see things eye to eye.

There have been a few well-meaning saints who have debated with me the fact any attempt to explain a person's temperament is wrong. They assume by understanding a person's temperament only gives birth to excuses. But I respectfully disagree. Empathy is not always the same as sympathy. This book is my way of answering why we should study temperaments. Just like a psychiatrist studies his patient to understand why he or she behaves the way they do, we too should study a person's temperament disposition to have a healthier understanding of why people act the way they do. Since studying human temperaments I'm now much more tolerant with people when we differ than before.

Probably the first thing you need to realize is that an average person has two predominate temperaments, which govern and guide his or her idiosyncrasies. Usually one of the two temperaments will take charge and control a person's main behavior and conduct. But when a person has two temperaments that are the exact opposite of each other, the person often finds himself or herself having a difficult time making up their mind. What has seized in their mind is nothing more than their temperaments fighting against one another. One temperament is telling them to do one thing while the other is telling them something totally different. And this example also holds true when two people who have an exact opposite temperament discuss an issue.

Take me for an example. I'm a strong sanguine with phlegmatic as my secondary temperament. On my temperament testing score I came up with only a touch of melancholy and choleric. On the sanguine side of my temperament I am a super extrovert who loves being the center of attention while at the same time my phlegmatic side is a super introvert, which is calm, shy, and unexcited. Two exact opposite super temperaments that constantly fight against one another. Since opposites attract each other in marriage this example hopefully helps explain the reason why so many couples almost never see eye to eye.

Another example would be when early in marriage I tried to wear the shoes of a choleric before realizing they would never fit. I quickly ran into the problem of trying to find a pair that would match my personality. I couldn't find a pair to go with any of my outfits. Every choleric pair of shoes I tried on would be either too big or small and none were comfortable. They would make my feet swell, smell, and hurt because they were too tight. It didn't matter if I stretched them to make them conform to my feet I was never able to walk comfortably in a choleric's shoe. I finally tried on a corrective pair. I remember shortly after Kathy and I were married we had one of those newlywed

Chapter 8

disagreements. I discussed the issue with a church member (which today I understand is a huge no-no!) Never discuss family matters with an outsider. "It is not safe to permit the least departure from the strictest integrity." When a person relates a family issue, or complains to another person, they violate their marriage vows and dishonor their mate by breaking down the wall erected to preserve the sanctity of the marriage relation. This only throws wide open the door and invites Satan to enter with his insidious temptations. And this is just as Satan would have it.[9] The church member suggested that I was the man of the household and should wear the pants. "Stand up! Be a man and take charge!" was his counsel. Well, I did. Needless to say, a phlegmatic standing up to a choleric is like a mouse standing up to a lion. The issues usually only worsen. Mainly because a phlegmatic will back down before he has a chance to speak. They will practice their speech before a mirror, work up the courage and step forward but freeze before they utter many words when they look into the eyes of a choleric. And this is exactly what I did. I spoke up for about a minute until Kathy looked at me with those eyes only a choleric has and I quietly backed off and returned my corrective choleric shoes.

Now the issue here is not what is right or wrong. The principle I'm trying to make is not who the Bible says is to rule the household. The conclusion I'm wanting to suggest is how different temperaments react to another. We will look at this in more detail later and I'll share more ideas on how different temperaments respond to one another.

All those closely acquainted with me know I usually wear western boots. I love western boots so much that someday I'm going to preach a sermon titled, "When I die, bury me in Texas with my boots on." I have no idea what the sermon will be about, but I like the title. I walk, preach, teach, do just about everything but sleep and swim in them. And I'm waiting for the day when someone will invent a swimming and sleeping pair. Boots and I are perfect together. With my west Texas accent we click, blend, and make a great team. I feel out of place when wearing anything else on my feet. I'll even be glad when someone designs a jogging pair.

This example also demonstrates temperament blends. Some temperament blends are natural and compliment each other. While on the other hand, some blends can constantly be at battle with each other. They run aground and sink because they cannot work together as a team. One temperament wants to take charge and demand to wear the pants. This comes as natural to them as it is for rabbits to multiply. And unless they have undergone the born-again experience, a battle of temperaments will take place.

This is the very reason why Kathy and I often ram our heads and lock horns on almost every issue we discuss. Our thinking is as different as daylight is to nighttime. However, because of the born-again experience we have both experienced, even though at times it is not always easy, we now endeavor to accept the other one's feelings.

We could look at marriage attraction this way. God designed our temperaments to work like a magnet. One principle characteristic of magnets is that the North Pole of one magnet attracts the South Pole of another magnet, but it repels the North Pole of another magnet. That is, unlike poles attract each other, and like poles repel each other. I have never met a married couple that has the exact same temperaments. They might have one temperament close to each other but you can bet that his or her other temperament will be the opposite.

You may recall the computer-dating craze of the 70's. The so-called match makers tried to team two people together with their likes and dislikes. Today we know many of the couples who fell in love and got married didn't last long together. I once read a story about a new kind of computer "bug" that was programmed with all your likes and dislikes. You were to wear it on your belt so if you got close enough to someone who had a "bug" with the same likes and dislikes as yourself, then the bug would go off telling you the prefect mate of your dreams just passed by.

Chapter 8

Have you ever noticed our best friends are usually of the same temperament as ourselves? We have the same likes and dislikes. We have so much fun with our friends. They understand us. This could explain why we often find it easier to talk to friends about things that bother us than we do our spouse. The problem is we don't marry our best friends. That is why God brings two completely different people together to form a whole and complete couple. The two shall become one. "For this cause shall a man leave his father and mother, and shall be joined unto his wife, and they two shall be one flesh" Ephesians 5:31.

No married couple is exempt from attacks by the enemy. There is evidence all around us that the devil is hard at work breaking up homes. We must take Peter's advice seriously. "Casting all your care upon him; for he careth for you. Be sober, be vigilant; because your adversary the devil, as a roaring lion, walketh about, seeking whom he may devour" 1 Peter 5:7,8. "While men are ignorant of his devices, this vigilant foe is upon their track every moment. He is intruding his presence in every department of the household,...perplexing, deceiving, seducing, everywhere ruining the souls and bodies of men, women, and children, breaking up families... And the Christian world seem to regard these things as though God had appointed them and they must exist.

"Satan is continually seeking to overcome the people of God by breaking down the barriers which separate them from the world."[10] He attacks when and where we least expect it. I did not have to give many marriage counseling discussions before I discovered one huge area the enemy often directs his attention toward. That area is time. Most couples are not taking time for the other. I've uncovered the sad fact that all we accomplish when we don't "take time for two" is the spark of marriage quickly leaves.

Years ago I decided to use only good gasoline in my automobiles. It doesn't mattered to me I have to pay more. By doing this I receive better mileage and far fewer engine repairs. My fuel-injectors stay cleaner and last longer. It saves wear and tear of the mechanism of the motor. But the one area I have found by running good gas is so beneficial is the fewer spark plugs I have to replace. And because of their engine and body design, I have two autos that are very expensive to replace the plugs.

I usually stick with a certain brand of gas I like and trust. There have been the occasions when I tried another brand and was sorry before I got very far down the road. If we would learn to check the gas (attitude) of our marriage, we would have far less repairs than we do now.

Today we live in an age of self-service gas stations. We check our own air, oil, tires, and batteries. We make the decision of what and when to check under the hood. And because of this, many automobiles go unattended and neglected. Some of you may remember the "good ole' days" when we had full service gas station. It was a time when a gas station attendant would quickly run up to your window and ask, "Fill her up?" Then they would proceed to check under your hood and if you needed oil or a new belt they would kindly inform you. You always got your windows washed and your tires aired up. As you drove away you felt at ease knowing your car was in tip-top shape and ready to endure any road hazard that might come your way.

If we would learn to check under the hood of our marriages daily, fill up with only the best of fuels, we would find many repairs could be avoided. In other words, do nice things for each other. Go out to eat. Take a moment to relax and just talk. Surprise each other with gifts for no reason. Take a second honeymoon. Take the kids to the babysitters and go to the mall or play a game of mini-golf.

Someone might be thinking, "Well that sounds great but running better gasoline can get expensive." But my friend, have you priced what marriage counseling costs nowadays? Not only that, have you taken into account what a divorce costs? Believe me you will shell out thousands on divorce settlements and child support. Divorces are very expensive and unless you have a lot of money you want to throw away, you can't afford not to run a better grade of gas in your marriage and check under the hood daily. Rotate the tires of your marriage and keep them properly aired and you will find they will wear very slowly if at all.

How do you keep your marriage in check? Do you find it difficult to understand your mate? Are temperaments still new to you? Perhaps the next chapter will help.

Chapter 9

"Determinations"

Several years back while working in the Iowa - Missouri Conference, I, along with some other pastors, had been asked (some recruited) if we would assist erecting a red water slide for our summer camp. One of our assignments besides assembling the water slide was to build a new wooden deck at the entrance of it. The treated wood we were to use was expensive and required each piece to be screwed down. Now the truth was, most of the pastors there knew nothing or very little about carpentry work. (Including me). Oh, sure some of us had assisted enough in building church sanctuaries that we knew how to use a hammer and power saws, but that was about the total sum of it. There was only one pastor who had any real skill in knowing how to read a blueprint and build. He had been a carpenter before he entered the ministry and was quickly appointed as the one in charge of the decking project. One of his job duties was to see to it the rest of us knew what we were doing. One thing for sure, even though most of us didn't have a clue how to build a deck, he did. He must have been a melancholy, because everything had to be perfect. If it didn't fit exact, he would have us unscrew the plank and cut another one. The screw holes even had to be measured just so far apart, which drove us sanguines crazy. Everything was running smoothly as Big Red was slowly coming together for that summer's run of young people to enjoy. Then one of the Missouri pastors, Keith, asked if he could try his hand at screwing in some of the flooring using the cordless drill. He started having trouble from the very start. For some reason, Pastor Keith couldn't get the hang of burying the screw heads into the wood. Each time he tried his drill bit would

Chapter 9

slide off of the screw placing a deep cut in the new wood. This didn't set lightly with the pastor in charge so he advised him to bear down a little harder placing his weight on the center of the drill until the bit came to a complete stop.

Well after a few endeavoring tries and not wanting to give up, Pastor Keith got the hang of it, and off he went placing each screw in its right spot. The rhythm of hearing Keith's screw gun became almost routine. Later as the rest of us were doing our assignments, we couldn't help but notice that Keith's pattern of screwing had suddenly changed. He appeared to be bearing down on one certain screw longer than usual. The screw would not bury its head and bring the drill bit to a stop. It just kept turning and turning. Finally someone said, "Keith, stop. Something is wrong."

When he stopped and brought the drill bit up, we all started laughing. Keith had remained bearing down on the screw until he welded the bit and "broken" screw together. He was "determined" that the bit was going to stop turning before he was going to stop screwing. He was about to throw the bit away when I asked if I could have it. I still have that welded drill bit and screw in my office today. I have it taped to a three by five card with the word "DETERMINATION" in bold letters printed on it. Whenever I look at it I am reminded of Pastor Keith's determination to keep going and not quit, no matter what.

I wonder, are you "determined" and settled to make your marriage work and not quit no matter what the cost? "If thy brother trespass against thee, rebuke him; and if he repent, forgive him. And if he trespasses against thee seven times in a day, and seven times in a day turn again to thee, saying, I repent; thou shalt forgive him." Luke 17:3, 4. "And not only seven times, but seventy times seven—just as often as God forgives you."[1] You must determine in your heart from this point on to make your marriage work. It should not be our concern to judge whether our spouse has truly repented of the pain they may have caused us. Our concern and duty is to forgive. "Christians, in their dealing with one another, are to be controlled by principles of mercy and love...The duty of every Christian is plainly outlined in the words: 'Judge not, and ye shall not be judged: condemn not, and ye shall not be condemned: forgive, and ye shall be forgiven: give, and it shall be given unto you; good measure, pressed down, and shaken together, and running over.' 'As ye would that men should do to you, do ye also to them likewise.' These are the principles that we shall do well to cherish."[2] You will find more on forgiveness in the chapter "The Storms of Marriage." For right now I would like to discuss more about your determination to make your marriage work.

Thomas Edison tried over and over before he came across the formula that worked to invent the light bulb. Edison did not succeed his first try or his second; in fact, he did not even succeed on his 2,999th attempt. It wasn't until his 3,000th time did he find success. Each time he tried, Edison learned a little more on what worked and what did not work. I'm sure there were the moments when he probably felt a little discouraged but he never gave up. When something didn't perform the way he wanted it to, he tried something else. Around his 1,500th failed experiment a reporter asked him if he shouldn't give up and acknowledged that it's impossible to make a light bulb. To this Edison replied, "Young man, I have not failed 1,500 times. To the contrary, I have successfully identified 1,500 ways that will not work to make a light bulb."

A happy successful marriage is a lot like that. It's a learning process. One day at a time. When something didn't worked for Thomas Edison, he changed the parameters a little and tried again. We must do the same with developing a happy marriage. We must never fail to realize that a complete and happy marriage is a process, which takes time. Becoming discouraged when something doesn't work will only hinder the progress that has been made. We must not think we've failed when something we tried didn't work. It's like the first time I fell off while riding a horse. What did I do? I brushed off the dirt and got back on. (Later I asked mom to kiss the wounds but that's another story). As long as we learn from each effort, then each effort will be

Chapter 9

successful. Each attempt toward making our marriage better is a steppingstone to success and happiness.

Most will say married life is tough these days. At times we are tempted to give up. It's not easy being caught between financially tight shoestring budgets and unreachable demands from our spouse, family, and kids. Marriage these days have many obstacles to jump over. Trying to jump over obstacles alone isn't easy. We need each other to keep the other one strong. "Though difficulties, perplexities, and discouragements may arise, let neither husband nor wife harbor the thought that their union is a mistake or a disappointment. *Determine to be all that it is possible to be to each other.* Continue the early attentions. In every way encourage each other in fighting the battles of life. *Study to advance the happiness of each other.* Let there be mutual love, mutual forbearance. Then marriage, instead of being the end of love, will be as it were the very beginning of love. The warmth of true friendship, the love that binds heart to heart, is a foretaste of the joys of heaven."[3]

You may have to try a variety of different approaches in getting the message across that your love for your spouse is so strong that you are determined to make your marriage work no matter what the cost. Anytime someone conducts an experiment of any kind, they must first believe the product can be made. If you want your marriage to be happy then you have to believe it can be achieved.

Learning to show appreciation to your spouse doesn't necessarily mean you have to approve of every decision they make. It also doesn't mean you have to praise everything they do. But being sensitive to their needs and knowing how to approach them when they have done something which has aggravated you is very important to master.

Most married couples who come to me for counseling seem to fear having a happy marriage will be impossible for them to ever achieve. For some reason these couples tend to believe their marriage is hopeless and God's promises are not intended for them. They perceive those promises are for the "saints" or "spiritual giants" of the church. If God's promises were intended for their marriage, they reason, we would not be having the problems we are experiencing. But I want to assure every married individual, no matter how hopeless your marriage may seem at this moment, the Lord's promises of having a happier marriage here on this earth were written just for you! Regardless of how discouraged you may feel right now, you can overcome the hardships and obstacles that are standing in your way.

It doesn't matter how complex and difficult your marriage may be at this time, God can unravel and repair it. No matter how difficult your spouse may be to understand, God can give you strength to accept them for who they are. Accept the fact there is nothing too difficult for God. "If you come to God, feeling helpless and dependent, as you really are, and in humble, trusting prayer make your wants known to Him whose knowledge is infinite, who sees everything in creation and who governs everything by His will and word, He can and will attend to your cry, and will let light shine into your heart and all around you;... You may have no remarkable evidence at the time that the face of your Redeemer is bending over you in compassion and love, but this is even so. You may not feel His visible touch, but His hand is upon you in love and pitying tenderness.

"God loves...you and wants to save you with an abundant salvation. But it must not be in your way, but in God's own appointed way. You must comply with the conditions laid down in the Scriptures of truth, and God will as surely fulfill on His part as His throne is sure."[4] How is your determination holding up today?

Chapter 10

"Mask or Not to Mask; That is the Question"

"A noble, all-round character is not inherited. It does not come to us by accident. A noble character is earned by individual effort through the merits and grace of Christ. God gives the talents, the powers of the mind; we form the character... Conflict after conflict must be waged against hereditary tendencies... A character formed according to the divine likeness is the only treasure that we can take from this world to the next."[1] "The old nature, born of blood and the will of the flesh, cannot inherit the kingdom of God. The old ways, the hereditary tendencies, the former habits, must be given up; for grace is not inherited. The new birth consists in having new motives, new tastes, new tendencies."[2]

Whenever I work with anyone who is having emotional problems I try to watch his or her body language and eyes. Body language speaks loud and clear to what one is feeling inside and is a useful tool in counseling. I've come to believe body language also speaks a little about what temperament a person is. For example, I've noticed many cholerics look straight in my eye and sit up straight. They hold a cold look on their face giving off the message they feel it is pointless being here. Phlegmatics have the tendency to look around the room and slump down in their chair giving me an indication they do not want to be there and talk very little. Sanguines and melancholies tend to look at one object and stare. They often look sad, depressed, dejected, and discouraged. They seldom allow their eyes to look directly at their spouse, that is, if they happen to be there, which is usually not the case.

A Powerful Marriage

I recall the original sin with our first parents. This illustrates the breakdown, which often comes between two people with distrust and hurt of blaming each other for their own wrongdoing. When God asked Adam what he had done, he blamed Eve for his sin. Eve blamed God for making the snake. When God called they both ran and hid themselves. Not just once, but twice. Once in the forest and the other behind some fig leaves. They had hoped the fig leaves would hide their shameful state. But to me it was nothing more than a mask. A cover up to convince God all was OK. From that day on mankind has been running and hiding from God, hiding behind masks hoping to convince God and the world all is OK.

It doesn't matter what temperament we are; we all have worn masks at some time or another. A mask is nothing more than a cover up of mascara of what we feel inside. I find it sad when a denomination such as ours, which is so much against wearing make-up of any kind, wears more cosmetic masks on Sabbath than any other day of the week. We walk in church smiling and greeting each brother and sister we meet. The mask says loud and clear we are happy. No problems in my life. We hug and shake each other's hand while declaring "it is a glorious day to be alive." But if the truth were told, it would be a different story. Behind the mask we might find the children are unruly or in trouble with the law. The spouse is drinking or running around. There's not enough money to pay this month's bills. The doctor just discovered a lump. The company just announced a layoff. On and on the endless list continues.

The temperament, which appears to hide behind more masks than any other, is the melancholy. Melancholies often wear this "I'm so happy face" where the real truth is they are miserable inside. Because of their acting skills, I have often guessed a melancholy as a sanguine when we first meet. An average melancholy must have others think they are cheerful and everything is all right in their life. Recently I visited an evangelistic series being held in a district where I had once been the pastor. One of the members had also been a

Chapter 10

counselee of mine for two years. When I walked into the children's department I saw her just playing with the kids and looking so happy. But the moment she saw me she broke down and cried in my arms. The mask she wore told the world she was happy, but behind her disguise laid the truth: she was depressed, sad, and ready to give up.

Let's use the illustration of a woman wearing a lot of make-up to demonstrate more about mask wearing. Have you ever seen a woman overdoing the mascara, color toning, lipstick, and jewelry around her neck with rings on every finger? Often a woman dressed liked this is dubbed a "Jezebel." You may recall this is the way the Bible describes the evil Queen Jezebel. She was a woman decked out from head to toe with jewelry and makeup to make her appear more attractive. This is also similar to how Revelation 17 describes the false church. A false church appearance is nothing more than a mask pretending to be the true church. Now I don't mean to sound disrespectful, but when I picture a woman who wears a lot of makeup I think of Tammy Faye Baker. Every show on television her face was plastered with a covering of cosmetic war paint that made her look as if she was going to battle. I once heard of a white T-shirt, which had a huge black smudge blot on it with the words "I ran into Tammy Faye Baker at the mall today." When she cried on television her mascara ran down her face like rivers of black oil coming straight from an oil well. She must have thought wearing that much make-up made her look attractive. Maybe Jim Baker was enraptured with this sort of beauty, but not many men have found her outward adornment attractive. Now, I've never tested her, and I may be wrong, but I can't help but believe she was trying to hide behind a mask. (No pun intended).

Counseling and ministering has taught me, some women who wear this much make-up are actually hiding behind their true feelings. She does not want others to notice her hurt, grief, and pain that shadow her everyday life. She is unintentionally advertising the mourning, grief, and shame she is experiencing.

Counseling many melancholies has revealed they have the problem of believing that God cannot fully forgive them of their sins. For some reason they forget 1 John 1:9 teaches God clearly forgives everyone of all sin. "If we confess our sins, he is faithful and just to forgive us our sins, and to cleanse us from *all* unrighteousness" (*Emphasis added*).

In the volume, *Re-bonding* by Dr. Donald M. Joy, you'll find the story about a man named, Dr. Emmett Holt, Sr. who wrote a book called, *The Care and Feeding of Children*. In this edition he taught that it would be better if a person wouldn't touch or hold newborns when they cried or needed their diaper changed. He urged parents not to rock or cradle their babies. He claimed it is best only to feed them on a timed schedule and preferably from a bottle. I respectfully disagree with Dr. Holt. I believe every living thing God created needs and wants to be held and loved.

My family once had a cat named, Cookie. From the day we brought her home we discovered she wasn't a very loveable cat. Like most cats she picked and chose her moments when she wanted to be loved. I recall the time when she was about to have a litter of kittens. She was having a hard time delivering so the family (my vote didn't count) decided I should be the mid-wife and help in the delivery. I had never seen a "live" birth before. Oh sure I knew how baby kittens were born; I had seen the videos on television and at school; I knew what takes place. But to actually be there in person is another story.

I could tell Cookie was having a hard time delivering the first kitten and knew what I had to do, help her. At first I stroked her back and said the only words I could think of when a mother is about to give birth; "Come on, you can do it. Take deep breaths. Push, push." Well that didn't help much. The baby kitten was stuck about half way out with no progress-taking place. I knew I would have to reach down and take the baby kitten by the head and pull. I remember tugging and saying; "Lord, please don't let me pull this baby kitten's head off." I was pulling hard or so it seemed. Finally the first kitten released her hold and decided maybe if she

Chapter 10

didn't want her head pulled off she better come on out. I wasn't prepared for what happened next. Cookie did what came naturally and licked her first born to life and ate the placenta. Needless to say, I was feeling a little sick. Yet, I was also feeling like a brand new daddy! I continued to stroke Cookie's back as she prepared for the next one to be born. With each stroke Cookie looked up at me as if to say; "Thank you for your help." A bond came between her and me at that moment which had never been there before. From that day on, Cookie would come to me to love and stroke her back. Something she had rarely ever done before. I came to love that cat probably more than any cat we have ever owned. It just took some time for her to figure out she needed touching and loving too.

Everyone at sometime or another wants and needs to be touched, cuddled, and loved. Cats, dogs, adults, and children. I think of the stories I've heard about AIDS patients who expressed how nice it would be if someone would touch them. Since they contracted their deadly disease, most people won't come close to them. No doubt you've heard the true story, which took place in a nursery orphanage. Many physically healthy babies were mysteriously dying. No one could explain the deaths of these children who were well fed. One day someone observed that the children who lived were the ones that were being held and loved more than the ones, which were not cuddled as often. The orphanage hired women to hold and cuddle *all* the babies as any mother would hold and love their own. The mystery was solved. Why? Because humans (and animals) of all size, shape, and age need and want to be loved.

For this reason, verses like Romans 8:35, 38, 39 mean so much to me; "Who shall separate us from the love of Christ? shall tribulation, or distress, or persecution, or famine, or nakedness, or peril, or sword?... For I am persuaded, that neither death, nor life, nor angels, nor principalities, nor powers, nor things present, nor things to come, Nor height, nor depth, nor any other creature, shall be able to separate us from the love of God, which is in Christ Jesus our Lord."

The Bible declares "God is love" and has never stopped loving any of us no matter what we have done in the past or will do in the future. I'm convinced that God will never stop loving any of His children, even those who never accept Him. "Can a woman forget her sucking child, that she should not have compassion on the son of her womb? yea, they may forget, yet will I not forget thee. Behold, I have graven thee upon the palms of my hands..." Isaiah 49:15,16. "The marks of the crucifixion in the hands and feet of our Lord are evidences that Christ has not forgotten his people. He has bought them, and the ransom has been paid. Jesus, the world's Redeemer, *knows all his children by name*, and on those who believe shall come the glory of God."[3] Just think, our names will forever be engraved on the palms of His hands.

I have witnessed many of my counselees wearing a mask on Sabbath morning hoping to convince others how happy they are. But the truth is they are only fooling themselves. I've even tried it a few times myself but soon realized it doesn't always work. I'll never forget the time when we had just come home from church and my daughter said to me; "Dad, you act one way around church members and another way at home." Ouch! Double ouch!! That hurt and cut me deep. I was wounded from my head to my feet. I thought, what could she possibly mean? I only wish I knew then what I know now that the best way to alienate any young person from Christ, His church, and yourself, is fail to live at home what you profess and preach at church.

This made me look and feel like a Christian hypocrite. Which I guess I was. I wasn't portraying a good example. If our example is inconsistent with what we preach, then that makes us a deceiver and a mask wearer. "A genuine conversion changes hereditary and cultivated tendencies to wrong."[4]

I believe one of the most positive things that we can do to set a good example is to let our family see we act the same at home, church, play, and work. Let them see Christ lives in us. Albert Schweitzer once said the three best ways to teach our family was: "First example. Second example. Third example." Great, now he tells me! Where was he when I needed his advice? In essence, I finally realized I could not expect my family to rise spiritually any higher than the example I set before them.

It was after my daughter spoke these words to me that I started really looking at my Christian experience. Could I be one way at home and a completely different way around my church family? As much as it hurts to type this, I'm afraid my daughter was right. I was two completely different persons and I knew I had to take off one of those masks. But which one? Should I act at home the way I do at church or act at church the way I do at home? Or was the answer I must let Christ take full control of my life and transform me into His image? I believe the answer is obvious. When Christ has taken over our life, any mask we wear can be removed and the real person can come out. Today, the person people see is the real me. Mistakes and all. They see a person who now is in the hands of the Potter, being reshaped into His likeness. The face, which is now seen, is the face of a new recreated, born again child of God. Jesus declares, "Behold, I make all things new" Revelation 21:5. "Therefore if any man be in Christ, he is a new creature: old things are passed away; behold, all things are become new" 2 Corinthians 5:17. At the end of this chapter I have given you the road map from God's Word on how you too can become a new creature in Jesus.

I feel everyone should act as natural as possible and be himself or herself around others. We should never be someone we're not. Trying to wear another personality other than your own is as unnatural as trying to wear someone's false teeth, and probably just as nauseating. Many times I get to meet people away from church and discover they're not as happy as they seem on Sabbath morning. I get to see the real person away from their happy church mask. What many do not realize is their imitation and artificial personality is hard to sell to everyone. Angels always know the truth and record what we say and do.

Whether at church or at home. "There is altogether too much careless talking, censuring, fault-finding, in families that profess to love and serve God. The unkind words, the irreverence and disrespect, found in many families make angels weep. What a record is made upon the books of heaven of unkind looks and words that bite and sting like an adder. And this is not the record of one day in the year merely, but of day after day. Oh that these families would consider that angels of God are taking a daguerreotype of the character just as accurately as the artist takes the likeness of the human features; and that it is from this that we are to be judged."[5]

If you should ask me if everything is OK and I say, "Yes all is great," when everything is not great, isn't that lying? Now don't take that the wrong way. There are times when we should not reveal personal or family problems. Some personal and all family problems should not be disclosed to just anyone. But is it wrong to say something has happened and you seek their prayers without having to always go into details? I don't think so. "Often prayer is solicited for the afflicted, the sorrowful, the discouraged; and this is right. We should pray that God will shed light into the darkened mind and comfort the sorrowful heart."[6] Isn't God's house of worship His hospital for sinners and those in pain?

Hanging in our kitchen today is a charming wooden MISSISSIPPI WEATHER GUIDE, which a friend of ours from Iowa gave us. It came with these simple instructions: "Hang outside and Check Daily. If the Rope is Dry – Fair. Rope Wet – Raining. Rope Moving – Windy. Rope White – Snowing. Rope Gone – Tornado." Cute but hopefully you realize each forecast is true.

I was looking at the weather guide one morning and thought; you know, having a happy home should work the same way. There are sure signs, which foretell when something is wrong. For example when a melancholy seems to be in his or her own little world and doesn't want to communicate, this is a sure sign that something is bothering them. When a sanguine isn't smiling and telling jokes, you know something has taken place in their life. That's a signal warning a storm of great magnitude has erupted in his life. If the choleric is not directing and trying to take control of different activities, if they just sit in the corner and give no input, you can rest assure that some sort of severe storm has brewed up somewhere in their life. If a phlegmatic stops keeping a cool head when situations come their way, it too is a positive indication that a storm has rolled into their life. Each temperament can give signals when something has happened in his or her world. Each signal or warning sign indicates something has turned them around from their normal self. We must learn to watch for these warning signs in our families.

After careful consideration I came up with my own simple **HAPPY MARRIAGE GUIDE:** "Check it daily!" This is about the most important and best instruction I can give on how to have a happy marriage. Watch daily for warning signs that a problem might be brewing up in your marriage. Then treat the signs as a real warning a storm has hit. Learning to read our spouse's signs and body language can go a long way toward healing a hurt or preventing a storm. "'We are laborers together with God.' 1 Corinthians 3:9... Each one is to stand in his watchtower, listening attentively to that which the Spirit has to say to him, remembering that his every word and act makes an impression, not only on his own character, but on the characters of those with whom he is connected."[7]

Shortly after Kathy and I were married, she and Tonya came home from shopping one afternoon. I met them at the door as usual, but this time Kathy walked right past me without a hello or kiss. From the look in her eyes I knew a storm had hit. When Tonya came in I asked, "What's up?" She said mother had received a ticket for having an expired license tag. Seeing that the tags were kept up to date was my responsibility, and I had failed my responsibility by not watching the date. Needless to say, Kathy was very upset with me. After praying, I believe God gave me the right words to say. I told her I was sorry and offered to go down and pay the ticket myself. It was like Jesus calming the storm all over again. Kathy's look on her face changed instantly from red with anger to normal with forgiveness. She knew I had not intentionally forgotten to purchase new car tags. She forgave me and the tempest became peaceful. I saw a warning sign when she walked in the house and I acted upon it in the right away, which calmed the gale before it grew into a hurricane. If any good came out of that ordeal it is this, I have never failed again to purchase car tags before they expire.

Let's face the facts; there will probably always be disagreements between husbands and wives. But as far as possible without sacrificing and compromising our Christian principles, finding a middle course to demonstrate our love and to keep peace in the family is always beneficial. I'm a firm believer that it's not so much what you say but how you say it that makes the difference. I could have laughed about Kathy getting stopped, but what would the outcome have been then? I shudder to think about it.

Another good demonstration to explain masks comes from a story I read which went something like this. A preacher and his wife were traveling on vacation and on Sabbath they visited the local church and discovered the church was between pastors. With no speaker arranged to speak that morning the congregation asked the preacher if he would speak, and he replied he would be most happy to. After a fabulous sermon the visiting pastor was shaking hands at the door when one of the older ladies of the church asked the pastor's wife if she preached too. She said; "No. My husband does the preaching, I'm the one that practices what he preaches." Ouch! Low blow! Yet, often so true. A living, practicing demonstration speaks louder than anything we say.

It's easy for some to get up on Sabbath morning and preach on Luke 17:4. "And if he trespass against thee seven times in a day, and seven times in a day turn again to thee, saying, I repent; thou shalt forgive him." It might be a strong and powerful sermon that transforms many. But if the preacher doesn't practice what he preaches, what good has he done for his family? Speaking from experience, I know it's not always easy to practice at home what I preach. My sermons are often spoken to me as much if not more than to my members. Let's paraphrase the verse above and bring it home. "If your spouse or children disappoint or hurt you seven times in one day, and seven times in the same day says 'I'm sorry'; then you should forgive them" (*The New David Farmer Revised Version*). Practicing what you preach is always the best teacher. If we learn to live what we teach and preach, our spouse and children might be more apt to listen to us when we speak. "The hearing ear, and the seeing eye, the LORD hath made even both of them" Proverbs 20:12.

I don't know why it is, it doesn't matter if we get up on the right side of the bed or not, but many of us still have the tendency to behave toward those outside the family better than we do our own spouse or children. It has always amazed me how we can act nicer to strangers than the one(s) we love the most. I'm a firm believer that the loving forgiving mask we wear around strangers or friends should first be worn at home.

It has been proven many times there is nothing, which handles a case of the gripes better than an afternoon walk. Nothing restores a bad outlook on life better than a visit to the local hospital. Nothing unites a couple better than a hug or kiss. And there is no better way to win the respect, approval, and affection of a friend, child, or spouse than to genuinely love them. People know a phony. Love wins when everything else fails. No one can win another's love and respect by knocking them down and fussing at them. Embarrassing or exploiting them in front of others has never gained any ground in improving one's relationship. No one is drawn to another when they have been threatened or given the cold shoulder. The only thing, which can thaw or draw is by loving them for who they are. Mistakes and all.

Love has a way of winning others when reasoning and scolding fail. Reasoning is often met with complete rejection. Scolding is apt to be met with blow for blow. Love finds hearts understanding. Why? For then they see no need to argue or strike back.

I have found many married couples in order to get along with the other, one or both start wearing a mask. Trying to "act" like someone they are not just to keep peace. But this has never been in God's plan. We are whom He made us. Mask wearing is not what He had in mind when He created any of us. Loving and accepting each other was what God had in mind.

During my teenage years I was dating a girl whose father owned a black 1959 Volkswagen. One evening we asked if we could borrow it to go riding around in. I'll never forget climbing into the driver's seat and looking for the gas gauge. It didn't have one. My girl friend's father got a huge laugh at my expense and then proceeded to show me a small lever in the middle of the baseboard that could be switched over to a small gasoline reserve tank which would carry the car another thirty or so miles if you ran out.

Today, I find many marriages are running on reserve. Their lever was switched over a long time ago and now the reserve itself is almost used up. Selfishness runs high while forgiveness runs low in many homes. Couples quit communicating with each other and seem to move apart from one another. The story is told of a couple that had been married for years and was driving home from church one Sabbath. The wife was on the passenger side of the front seat while the husband was driving. After a while she said; "Honey, remember when you used to sit by me when we were traveling? Now you sit on your side, and I sit on my side. What happened? How come we don't sit by each other anymore?" To this the gentleman replied; "Well, I haven't moved."

I have the bad habit of not always listening to my wife when she is speaking to me. Many times I may appear to be listening, looking directly at her, but my mind may be racing a hundred miles a minute trying to think of an excuse or instructions to give her instead of listening to what she has to say. I have hurt my wife time and time again because of this unfortunate tendency. Because of this unpleasant disposition of mine, I have developed the habit of biting the inside of my lower lip to remind me to listen and keep quite. If I find my mind drifting off, I'm quickly reminded that Kathy is talking because of the pain I have coming from the edge of my mouth.

Unfortunately I have the same tendency of not listening when God is speaking to me too. Often I catch myself not listening and find my mind drifting off trying to think of an excuse to give my Heavenly Father when He is communicating to me. There have been far too many times while reading His Word, and instead of listening to Him speak to me, I'm trying to justify why I did what I did or am about to do. "Few are listening for the voice of God, and ready to accept truth in whatever guise it may be presented."[8] "Many go away after listening to the most solemn messages of truth, and pursue the same careless, unsanctified course they did before, as though they had not heard the appeal of God to them. They go away and live to please themselves, live to suit their own fancy, in a way directly opposed to the way and will of God. We should not seek to follow our own way; we have had enough of that; it amounts only to weakness. We need to have the Holy Spirit of God with us moment by moment."[9]

To conclude this chapter let me say that it's not a sin to wear a mask. It's a sin to wear the wrong mask. Hypocritical behavior is saying one thing but doing another. In many areas of our lives and in many ways we avoid even trying to remove our mask because we do not want to experience the pain of failure. Some think in order for others to approve of them they must first feel good about themselves. But if we know who we are, we will not try to become someone we are not in order to feel value and meaning. Our self-image is determined not only by how we see ourselves but also by how we *think* others perceive us. We should never base our self worth on what we imagine others think of us and bow to the peer pressure of the world.

In Galatians 1:10, we find where Paul clearly identifies our search concerning approval: "For do I now persuade men, or God? or do I seek to please men? for if I yet pleased men, I should not be the servant of Christ." This passage explains why we can ultimately seek either the approval of men or the approval of God as the basis of our self-worth, but we cannot seek both.

Instead of wearing a mask, try being yourself. It's OK to let your loved ones know you have feelings that can be hurt. It's OK to let others know that you are human and make mistakes. After all, doesn't God allow us to let Him know how we feel? (See Psalms 13).

Here is what is commonly known as the Roman Road to Salvation. This is God's road map to full deliverance, pardon, and forgiveness of sin; the formula for removing a mask; God's Kleenex and prescribed antidote for cleaning away any covered mark of pain. It's His solution to hurt; His mirror in order to see ourselves the way He made us. As you look each verse up, let God speak to you. Allow Him to lead you into a full surrender of your heart. Keep in mind that nothing we do will save us. Salvation is free only through the shed blood of our Lord and Saviour, Jesus Christ.

1) Romans 3:10 - None righteous.
2) Romans 3:23 - For all have sinned.
3) Romans 5:12 - Death to all.
4) Romans 6:23 - God's gift is eternal life through Jesus Christ.
5) Romans 5:8 - Christ died for us while we were still sinners.
6) Romans 10:9 - Confess and believe in Jesus and be saved.
7) Romans 10:13 - Call upon Jesus and be saved.
8) Romans 4:5 – Our faith is accounted for righteousness.

Chapter 11

"Myths of a Happy or Miserable Marriage" [1]

Have you ever heard of the *National Enquirer*? Now, I didn't ask if you read the *National Enquirer* only have you heard of it. I once heard one of the supermarket tabloids had a headline, which read: *"New Discovery! Fat-Burning Prayers. Pray these prayers, and the pounds will melt away."* Forgive me but that is not the way I believe God works. If it were, then I would be the skinniest man in town. I heard of another tabloid, which reported that Rudolph the red nose reindeer had been found in someone's deep freezer. We probably all have seen the one about our national government being run by aliens from Mars. On and on headlines like these cover the checkout lanes at most supermarkets.

Many of us laugh at such funny and outrageous magazine articles. They're stupid and silly. Who in their right mind would believe some of the titles these grocery store newspapers have? But sad as it is to report many individuals around the country believe these types of articles or myths and have had their life messed up because of them. Numerous publications like these report Jesus is here walking among us at this very moment. He is healing and blessing people wherever He goes. For some reason grocery store tabloids seldom use Scripture to back up their claims. If people would only read what Revelation 1:7 says: "Behold, He is coming with clouds, and *every eye will see Him*" NKJV (*Emphasis added*). Or Matthew 24:27: "For as the lighting comes from the east and flashes to the west, so also will the coming of the Son of Man be" NJKV. No they want to gossip some hearsay from some hermit living in a cave in a country none of us have every heard of. And people buy it as the *"Gospel according to The National Enquirer."*

A Powerful Marriage

Then there are the myths, which appear to be harmless such as the Tooth Fairy, Santa Claus, and the Easter Bunny. Myths, traditions, and fables are everywhere we look, but probably the granddaddy tradition of them all is; we are to always have on a pair of clean underwear in case we are involved in an accident! I can just hear my mother now as I call her from the hospital to inform her I had been in an accident. The first question she asked; "Son did you put on a pair of clean underwear before you left the house this morning?" Yea, right Mom. Thanks for worrying about me!

No doubt many of you have heard of the phrase, "He's nothing more than a henpecked husband." When I started researching for this book, I made an absolute astounding discovery. I came to the conclusion the so-called "henpecked" man is nothing more than a phlegmatic man married to a choleric woman. She only *"appears"* to wear the pants of the family because she speaks louder than he does. Because of his easygoing temperament, he doesn't want to argue and debate the issue at hand. So he is labeled as weak and henpecked.

Which reminds me of a cute story I once heard over the radio. It seemed there once was this Christian couple, which wanted to see how many homes followed the Bible principle of allowing the man to be the head of the home. They wanted to know which way the scale would tip in most households, the man or the woman as head. One day they set out knocking on doors asking the question of who ruled and wore the pants of their house, the husband or wife? They had decided before they left that each home where the wife pronounced she wore the pants they would give a chicken. But to the homes where the man says he wears the pants they would give a horse.

As the day progressed into the afternoon they had given nothing away but chickens. They were starting to believe that every home in this city was governed and controlled by the wife. Finally late into the day they knocked on a door where a man answered. When the question was asked he replied, "Well I wear the pants here!" The couple was so delighted to have finally found a home that went by the Bible principle and acknowledged that the husband is to be the head of the household. They said, "Sir, we have a horse for you. Which would you like a black or white one?" The man thought about it for a few minutes and said, "I'll take a black one." At this a woman's voice in the back of the house could be heard; "No he won't. He'll take a white one!" The Christian couple said, "Never mind, we have a chicken for you instead."

Myths, harmless and stupid but let's face facts, they can be damaging. Some myths, which were taught to us as children, have stuck with us as adults. Do you still feel uneasy when a black cat walks in front of you? Do you ever avoid walking under a ladder or stepping on a crack on the sidewalk? How do you feel when you break a mirror?

I remember the time on my first Boy Scout campout the older scouts wanted to play a dirty trick on me. Acting as though they were doing their good deed for the day they informed me, the new Tenderfoot, that if I were bitten by more than three mosquitoes at any one time, I would die from lack of blood. And guess what? Several dozen dive-bombers bit me that evening after retiring for the night to my tent. I recall lying there waiting to die and talking to the Lord. I was repenting of my sins I had committed against Him for my whole life of eleven years. Boy, was I happy to wake up the next morning. Being the sanguine I am, I told everyone in camp I had beaten death. You should have seen the look on their faces.

This brings me to the purpose of this chapter, what about the myths of marriage. It has always been a mystery to me how two human beings who are so completely opposite in almost everything can be physically attracted to each other and falls in love. It is so complex and profound it cannot be understood merely in physiological terms. To even come close to understanding one would have to include the biological, psychological, spiritual, and the ethical dimensions of what bonds two people together to become one for life. This lifelong attachment that two people bring together to form one new entity, a corporate identity, will forever be studied and never be fully understood.

I shall never forget my "first true love" experience. Linda was her name. I was thirteen and she was a real cute twelve-year-old. We were living in west Texas and had just recently moved into the neighborhood where I became the new "boy" on the block. Linda, along with all of her brothers and sisters, wanting to show how neighborly they were, soon came over and knocked on our front door.

I answered the door and it was "love at first sight." She had the body of a fourteen-year-old with long blond hair and brown eyes. (Funny isn't it how we can remember all those details so many years ago yet find it difficult to remember our spouse's birthday or anniversary today!) We were both attracted to each other and the "puppy love" or "infatuation" as my folks wanted to call it started. Problem is, we had never heard of "puppy love" or "infatuation." All we knew was we were to spend the rest of our lives together.

My first "real" romance was never detoured by these demeaning labels. Let's face it, even today, demeaning labels tend to tell us more about the people who use them than about the people they think they are describing. The bond of love Linda and I had was indestructible by a tag our parents had placed on us.

Well you know "the rest of the story" as Paul Harvey would say. It's happened to most of us when we were young and in love. In a few weeks she found another and I wasn't her "only true love" anymore. I was heart broken to say the least. I tried everything to win her back. I bought her expensive gifts, you know, three-dollar bottles of perfume and five dollars a dozen roses. I tried calling her on the phone, but nothing seemed to work. And it wasn't long before I knew she was gone forever. It took me what seemed an eternity to get over her. But that week passed and I then found my "real" true love, Ronda. My love life continued like that until I found the one God had waiting for me. My really "real" first love, Kathy.

Chapter 11

In God's plan, when two people fall in love and get married, they form a new identity. "Wherefore they are no more twain, but one flesh" Matthew 19:6. They are no longer just plain so and so, they are now the husband or wife of so and so. In today's society it's not uncommon for a woman to keep her maiden name after marriage.

From the beginning, God planned two shall be formed into one. They were to leave their childhood home and form their own home together. God said the home was to be a blessing. "He ordained that men and women should be united in holy wedlock, to rear families whose members, crowned with honor, should be recognized as members of the family above. The family tie is the closest, the most tender and sacred, of any on earth. It was designed to be a blessing to mankind."[2]

But what happened? What went wrong? How could our perfect lover become just the opposite of the one we married? One reason is because most rush into marriage too soon. Listen to this counsel: "Marriage should be considered well before contracted."[3] "This question of marriage should be a study instead of a matter of impulse."[4] But how many people stop to think much about the one they are about to marry? From what I see, not many.

One myth I find which has done more damage is this one: "God did not bless our marriage. It was probably a mistake from the very beginning." Away with such thoughts. Remember, "What therefore God hath joined together, let not man put asunder" Matthew 19:6. As soon as thoughts like this creep into your marriage, it will be headed downhill. We must turn to God and ask Him to help us not to have such thoughts.

One of the most mystifying myths, which I know of, is why some women think they are no longer themselves when they get married. For some reason many women today think they lose their personal identity after saying "I do." This was a complete puzzle to me until I discovered the answer. Many husbands have made their wives feel that way. We men lead women into thinking they belong to us lock, stock, and barrel. They are no longer allowed to have their own personal identity because they are now our property. But does one lose their personal identity at marriage?

One author put this way. "She should remember that her marriage does not destroy her individuality."[5] "Your wife has just as much right to her opinion as you have to yours. Her marriage relation does not destroy her identity. She has an individual responsibility."[6]

"Our *personal identity* is preserved in the resurrection, …. The spirit, the character of man, (and woman) is returned to God, there to be preserved. In the resurrection every man (or woman) will have his own character… It (the body) lives again bearing the *same individuality of features*, so that friend will recognize friend."[7] One more. "Neither the husband nor the wife should merge his or her individuality in that of the other. Each has a personal relation to God. Of Him each is to ask, 'What is right?' 'What is wrong?' 'How may I best fulfill life's purpose?' Let the wealth of your affection flow forth to Him who gave His life for you. Make Christ first and last and best in everything. As your love for Him becomes deeper and stronger, your love for each other will be purified and strengthened."[8]

In heaven we will all have the same character, personality, temperament, and individuality as we develop now. But one problem I often find in many marriages is where one spouse is always trying to tell the other what to do. This causes big problems. As you will shortly see, we should never try to form our mates into something or someone they are not. That is God's job, not ours.

Who is Paul addressing in Ephesians 5:22–24? "Wives, submit yourselves unto your own husbands, as unto the Lord. For the husband is the head of the wife, even as Christ is the head of the church: and he is the Saviour of the body. Therefore as the church is subject unto Christ, so let the wives be to their own husbands in every thing."

Who is Paul addressing in Ephesians 5:25–33? "Husbands, love your wives, even as Christ also loved the church, and gave himself for it; That he might sanctify and cleanse it with the washing of water by the word, That he might present it to himself a glorious church, not having spot, or wrinkle, or any such thing; but that it should be holy and without blemish. So ought men to love their wives as their own bodies. He that loveth his wife loveth himself. For no man ever yet hated his own flesh; but nourisheth and cherisheth it, even as the Lord the church: For we are members of his body, of his flesh, and of his bones. For this cause shall a man leave his father and mother, and shall be joined unto his wife, and they two shall be one flesh. This is a great mystery: but I speak concerning Christ and the church. Nevertheless let every one of you in particular so love his wife even as himself; and the wife see that she reverence her husband."

He's addressing wives in verses 22–24 and husbands in verses 25–33. We cannot use those verses against each other. God is talking to one party and not the other. But what do we want to do? We want our spouse to read those verses and then demand they live up to them.

Right now if you should happen to be laid to rest, would you want to come up at the glorious Second Coming with the same character you have now concerning on how you treat your spouse? Would you want to treat your spouse in heaven the same way you treat them now? Do you let them be their own person? I once read a quote that went something like this. "How much of me would I have to change in order to make you happy? And how much of the original of me would be left?" Ouch! Double ouch!!

I remember the time when a wife of a friend of mine wanted to buy a used car from me for herself. She wanted this car badly. She kept it all night. Checked it out from top to bottom. Yep, it was the one she wanted. But her choleric husband said no. She didn't need another car. She could just keep the one she had. The problem I had wasn't that he wouldn't let her buy the car. The problem I had was that this woman worked and made a good living and had her own money. But he said no, she couldn't have it. There he sat

A Powerful Marriage

with a boat, racecar, and a few other fancy and expensive toys for himself. She had no say-so on whether he could have them or not. He completely ran her life.

We must learn to treat our loved one the way we would want to be treated. In Heaven and on the New Earth there will be no telling each other what to do and how to behave. If we can't accept our spouse for who they are today then how will we be able to in heaven? We need to ask God to change us into His perfect likeness, one that will accept our spouse the way they are. Now I didn't say we have to accept all the bad things our spouse does. Always remember that if God hates the sin but loves the sinner, shouldn't we also. "Charity hates the sin, but loves the sinner, and will warn him faithfully of his danger, pointing him to the Lamb of God who taketh away the sin of the world. Sin is not to be cloaked, but to be taken away. The love that is of heavenly birth is a resistless power, and it can be obtained only by a living connection with God. Would you move the hearts of men, you must come into actual contact with the God of love. God must first take hold of you if you would take hold of others."[9]

Before our spouse can change, we must change ourselves. They must see Christ in us first. We must forget the myth it is our spouse's duty to change before we are to change. God has never made a statement like that. "*Do not try to compel each other to do as you wish. You cannot do this and retain each other's love*. Manifestations of self-will destroy the peace and happiness of the home. *Let not your married life be one of contention. If you do you will both be unhappy.* Be kind in speech and gentle in action, *giving up your own wishes*. Watch well your words, for they have a powerful influence for good or for ill. Allow no sharpness to come into your voices. Bring into your united life the fragrance of Christlikeness."[10]

From the beginning, God made man and woman as individuals. Then He brought them together to become one. Neither man nor woman are to try to change the other into someone they are not. This is the job of the Holy Spirit. "In your life union your affections are to be tributary to each other's happiness. *Each is to minister to the happiness of the other*. This is the will of God concerning you. But while you are to *blend as one*, neither of you is to lose his or her *individuality in the other*. God is the owner of your individuality."[11]

Let me give you an illustration of what I mean by using the Holy Trinity as an example. You have the Father, Son, and Holy Spirit. Three completely different individuals, yet they are one in purpose and thoughts. Now before a man and woman become married to each other, they are two completely different individuals. But when they are married they become one. This must include their thoughts and purpose in life. They bring together their ideas, deeds, and personalities. They share their likes, dislikes, dreams, future, property, and everything else they hold in common with each other. Yet, they are still their own individual person.

The same holds true when we accept Christ into our life. His dreams, property, and entire kingdom are shared with us. We become partakers of His inheritance. "'And for this cause he is the mediator of the New Testament, that by means of death, for the redemption of the transgressions that were under the first testament, they which are called might receive the promise of eternal inheritance.' Heb.9:15 Christ died to purchase salvation for us. He was raised for our justification, and He ever lives to make intercession for us. His life and death bring salvation to every believing child of God. By His death we are reconciled to God; by His life, as it is wrought out in our life, we shall be saved. We may be poor in temporal things, but we are rich in the treasure that endures forever. We have the deeds to an *immortal inheritance*, the title papers to a life that measures with the life of God."[12] "The beautiful new earth, with all its glory, was the *eternal inheritance* of the saints. The kingdom and dominion, and the greatness of the kingdom under the whole heaven, was then given to the saints of the Most High, who were to possess it forever, even forever and ever."[13]

Most of us are sincere when we try to "improve" our spouse into becoming a better person. We believe that if only they could see themselves the way others and we see them then they would want to act differently. So we choose to help them whether they ask for our assistance or not.

A few years ago, Kathy and I were in San Antonio, Texas. We needed to purchase some items, so I asked the clerk if she would mind giving me directions to the closest Wal-Mart. I usually can follow directions pretty well, so I felt confident with her simple directions. We were to travel down the frontage road in front of the motel for a couple of miles and it would be on our right. She said, "You can't miss it."

After driving for about six or seven miles and not finding the Wal-Mart the clerk said, "I couldn't miss," I decided to try traveling down on the other side. Maybe I had misunderstood her directions. At the first turn around I came to was this mix master, spaghetti of roads crossing over and under each other. I made my turn under the overpass onto the other side and soon was headed the opposite direction I had been traveling. One thing was for sure; I just knew I was on the same frontage road just traveling the opposite way. But things looked different, I wasn't recognizing any of the landmarks. Kathy asked me if we were still on the same road and I assured her we were. I even became a little upset with her for even asking me such a question. I know my directions! We had been traveling west and we were now traveling east. So I thought.

After traveling for a while and not recognizing anything I had seen just a few minutes earlier, I saw something, which made me ill. The highway sign said I was on the wrong road-traveling south! And I had to turn to Kathy and say, "Honey, I'm on the wrong road." I won't write what she said.

The point is I was very sincere, but was sincerely wrong. If there is one thing I've discovered about having a happy marriage it is this. It takes more than sincerity to make a marriage work, it takes love. We may really be sincere in trying to change our spouse into someone they are not. But friends, we may be sincere, but we can also be sincerely wrong. Because it is not our duty to change the other. The Bible says, "Can the Ethiopian change his skin, or the leopard his spots? Then may ye also do good that are accustomed to do evil" Jeremiah 13:23. We may think we are doing God's good will when we try to "improve" our mates, but we are doing nothing more than driving them farther away from us.

If you want to believe Elvis is alive and doing well, then go ahead. If you want to believe in the Loch Ness Monster, I won't stop you. If you want to believe the moon is made of cheese or that the world is flat, then be my guest. But just because you believe in any or all of those doesn't make them true. Romans 1:25 says: "Instead of believing what they knew as the truth about God they deliberately chose to believe lies." Thinking we can change someone has been one of the most damaging beliefs and myths in marriages today. We cannot and dare not try to change anyone but ourselves.

God gives us the right and privilege to believe as we so choose. But that doesn't give us the right or privilege to try and change our spouse, kids, work mates, or family. This is a fable and myth. Whatever your spouse's temperament may be, no matter how tempting it is, you have no right to try and change them into behaving and acting like you want them to. If you think they're wrong, then you have the right to say how you feel. You have the right to say they have disappointed and hurt you. But even then, this must always be done in love.

Did you know our beliefs determine our behavior? I believe they do. Listen to Proverbs 4:23 from the NIV: "Above all else, guard your heart, for it is the wellspring of life." In other Words: "Be careful how you think. Because our life is shaped by our thoughts."

Did you know everything we do has an unconscious or conscious belief behind it? When you bought this book, did you stop to think if it would have anything printed in it? Probably not. We do so many little things everyday without thinking for one second about them. But then there are the times when we do stop and think before we leap. For example, you want to try out a new restaurant. You ask to see the menu. You find something that looks and sounds rather good. You ask yourself, "But is it?" You stop, think, and soon make a choice. I believe our beliefs about ourselves can also determine the way we act and behave. Even when the beliefs are wrong.

Let me give you another example of what I mean. If you are told you are clumsy, how will you act? Clumsy right. If you are told you are dump and stupid, how are you going to feel? Right again. Dump and stupid. And it's the same if you are told you are unlovable, cannot be trusted, and you make a lousy spouse. The list is endless. We act and behave the way we presume we are. And if is true and I believe it is, then isn't it also true for the way our spouse feels about himself or herself?

Take time to examine how you treat your spouse, kids, family and friends. I believe false beliefs about marriage can and often does cause emotional problems, stress, depression, worry and unhappiness. But when we have God in our heart and home, many of our emotional strains will disappear. I recently read that if you read every word that Jesus spoke in the New Testament you would make a very interesting discovery, Jesus said, *"I tell you the Truth"* over eighty times. He also says over twenty times *"Now you've heard it said, but I say to you."* What is Jesus saying to us? I believe He is exposing the myths concerning the Scriptures, which had misled many. But "If men would but take the Bible as it reads, if there were no false teachers to mislead and confuse their minds, a work would be accomplished that would make angels glad and that would bring into the fold of Christ thousands upon thousands who are now wandering in error. "[14]

Chapter 12

"The Y2Khaos of Marriage."

"After the creation of Adam every living creature was brought before him to receive its name; he saw that to each had been given a companion, but among them 'there was not found an help meet for him.' Among all the creatures that God had made on the earth, there was not one equal to man. And God said, 'It is not good that the man should be alone; I will make him an help meet for him.' Man was not made to dwell in solitude; he was to be a social being. Without companionship the beautiful scenes and delightful employments of Eden would have failed to yield perfect happiness. Even communion with angels could not have satisfied his desire for sympathy and companionship. There was none of the same nature to love and to be loved."[1]

Remember the fear of Y2K computer bug of January 01, 2000? Hopefully you realize if Y2K had achieved what some computer nerds were saying you might not be reading this book. If Y2K had infiltrated into our civilization of computerized living, then you might not have electricity, gas, and money in the bank right now.

I don't think we really realize just how dramatically computers have changed our lives. The words you are reading right now are being typed on my laptop. When we compare the way we do things with computers with the way we did things without them, the change is all the more startling. What I wouldn't have given for a computer or a calculator when I was in school! I was one of those students, which counted his fingers and toes to add numbers together. The calculator of my day was at my grandfather's office. It was a huge gray and blue adding machine with a pull handle on the side. Computers were only at NASA and in science fiction movies. In my childhood no one dreamed of the day when almost every home in America would have a personal computer, nor did anyone realize how computers would change our lives.

Many had predicted the Y2K computer bug would change our lives as we know it. It had people of every country around the world apprehensive with cold feet; the world was about to shut down and come to a complete stop. All because of older computers, which were never programmed, to read the dates, which have 00 at the end. Older computers will think it is the year 1900 instead of 2000. It's been very confusing to me. But I knew God was in control. He has been in control from the very beginning. He was in command when war broke out in heaven. "And there was war in heaven: Michael and his angels fought against the dragon; and the dragon fought and his angels, and prevailed not; neither was their place found any more in heaven. And the great dragon was cast out, that old serpent, called the Devil, and Satan, which deceiveth the whole world: he was cast out into the earth, and his angels were cast out with him" Revelation 12:7–9.

It was during this war in heaven when a "bug" called "sin" infiltrated this world with its programmer named, Lucifer, as its hacker. An all out assault with stealth technology against God's holy family was quickly launched. This rebel against God's creation instigated destroying everything God created and loved. A great controversy began between Christ and Satan over the character of God, His law, and His sovereignty in the universe. The devil introduced the spirit of rebellion first in heaven, later, into this world with Adam and Eve. The devil was so shrewd he came in the form of a talking snake to mislead Adam and Eve. He taught them to speak a total new language; the language of deceptiveness and this world became the theater of the universal conflict. "In order to accomplish his work unperceived, Satan chose to employ as his medium the serpent—a disguise well adapted for his purpose of deception. The serpent was then one of the wisest and most beautiful creatures on the earth…

Chapter 12

Resting in the rich-laden branches of the forbidden tree and regaling itself with the delicious fruit, it was an object to arrest the attention and delight the eye of the beholder. Thus in the garden of peace lurked the destroyer, watching for his prey."[2]

The devil lied and deceived Adam and Eve into believing that they would never die. "Now the serpent was more subtle than any beast of the field which the LORD God had made. And he said unto the woman, Yea, hath God said, Ye shall not eat of every tree of the garden? And the woman said unto the serpent, We may eat of the fruit of the trees of the garden: But of the fruit of the tree which is in the midst of the garden, God hath said, Ye shall not eat of it, neither shall ye touch it, lest ye die. And the serpent said unto the woman, Ye shall not surely die: For God doth know that in the day ye eat thereof, then your eyes shall be opened, and ye shall be as gods, knowing good and evil. And when the woman saw that the tree was good for food, and that it was pleasant to the eyes, and a tree to be desired to make one wise, she took of the fruit thereof, and did eat, and gave also unto her husband with her; and he did eat" Genesis 3:1–6.

After the devil was successful in achieving his goal of causing Adam and Eve to distrust God, he quickly commenced destroying the two institutions that would come out of the garden; the sacred vow of marriage and the Sabbath rest. "'Marriage is honorable' (Hebrews 13:4); it was one of the first gifts of God to man, and it is one of the two institutions that, after the Fall, Adam brought with him beyond the gates of Paradise."[3] We will look more at the Sabbath Rest God gave us in the next chapter.

The devil's main motive has always been to break our relationship, our communication off with God. To separate us from God like Eve separated herself from Adam in the garden. Communication was impossible while they were separated from one another. Neither knew the danger Eve was in and the trap being laid. Apart from God, we too are in danger of falling into Satan's traps.

The first argument between a husband and wife was in the garden. For the first time in their marriage they couldn't agree. They blamed each other and mankind has been doing the same every since. Husbands and wives have been pointing fingers and charging each other for their woes. One of the most common problems that couples complain to me about in counseling is they don't get along and see eye to eye. The problem is they can't understand the language the other one is using. A wall of miscommunication is between them.

The devil would love nothing more than to bring a language barrier "bug" in-between each married couple. He cherishes the moment he confuses the communication between a married couple to argue or worse, ask for a divorce. But divorce was never in God's plan for any marriage. "When the Pharisees afterward questioned Him concerning the lawfulness of divorce, Jesus pointed His hearers back to the marriage institution as ordained at creation. 'Because of the hardness of your hearts,' He said, Moses 'suffered you to put away your wives: but from the beginning it was not so' Matthew 19:8. He referred them to the blessed days of Eden, when God pronounced all things 'very good.' Then marriage and the Sabbath had their origin, twin institutions for the glory of God in the benefit of humanity. Then, as the Creator joined the hands of the holy pair in wedlock, saying, A man shall 'leave his father and his mother, and shall cleave unto his wife: and they shall be one' (Genesis 2:24), He enunciated the law of marriage for all the children of Adam to the close of time. That which the Eternal Father Himself had pronounced good was the law of highest blessing and development for man."[4]

This language barrier, which the devil used in the Garden of Eden, he still uses today. He not only confuses our language, but our hearing also. Have you ever said something only to have every word misconstrued? How is this when you know what you said and what you meant? The answer is simple: we all speak different languages, men, women, children, and temperaments. Do you recall in chapter 3 the statement; "The laws of genetics have reported that there are 300 billion possible chromosome combinations for human beings."[5] This means it is relatively impossible that two people could be the same. Each of us is as different as snowflakes and fingerprints. No two will ever see everything eye to eye nor speak the same dialect.

I've had the honor of traveling to Russia twice. Both times I picked up a little here and there on speaking Russian. I could say "Hello," "Good-bye," and "Thank you" in Russian, but that was about the length of it. I could never carry on any sort of conversation. Whenever a translator wasn't around, charades became the translator. You should have seen Pastor Tom Scull trying to get across we don't eat chicken. He had to dance around and cluck like a chicken while shaking his finger saying "Nyet." Trying to talk to someone of a different temperament or gender is much the same. We may have to act out what we are trying to say.

In Stu Weber's book, *Tender Warrior*[6], he explains how men and women speak a completely different dialect. Women speak "woman" and men speak "man." Simple to learn? Don't you believe it! Yet so true. There have been times when Kathy has tried hard to open up and explain her deep inner feelings to me. She tries to spell out what she needs from me, but it almost always ends up with the same line, "You just don't get it!" And she is right, I don't get it because I don't speak "woman." She and I constantly misinterpret each other's words and body language because neither speaks the other one's terminology. Our phraseology is as different as day and night. Both of our wording may mean the same thing but spoken from a different lingo than the other understands.

Not only do I not speak "woman," I don't speak her temperament idiosyncrasy either. Temperaments, like gender, cannot be understood by other temperaments. There are words, actions, looks, and feelings that can't be translated into another person's tongue. There are the times when I might smile at something while Kathy might frown at it. I might see humor in a joke, which she may interpret as in bad taste.

I recall the time I tried to explain to the Russians that I was from Iowa, the Hawkeye State. My translator turned to me and said Hawkeye could not be translated into Russian. The people wouldn't understand. Although that didn't make a bit of sense to me, we had to come up with another word the people could understand. This same principle applies when speaking to your mate. You might have to change your word(s) and find new expressions to convey your feelings. Your looks, actions, and choice of words all have something to do with communicating your true feelings.

During my seminars I often have questions on how to control a strong willed child or how to express one's feelings to their mate. I like to answer by suggesting they read different books by different authors. Authors have the tendency of writing in their temperament about things, which work for them. I despise authors, facilitators, and people who say, "If we will do it their way, everything will work out." This is simply not true as far as I am concerned. No one has the blueprints on another. Since we are all different, what works for you may not work for me. What is successful with one strong willed child may not be successful with the next and so on. Learning to speak each child and spouse's language is the most important thing a person can learn in how to communicate to each other. "A house with love in it, where love is expressed in *words and looks and deeds*, is a place where angels love to manifest their presence."[7] "*The looks, the tone of the voice, the actions,—all have their influence in making or marring the happiness of the domestic circle.* They are molding the temper and character of the children; they are inspiring or tending to destroy confidence and love. *All are made either better or worse, happy or miserable, by these influences.* We owe our families the knowledge of the word brought into practical life. All that it is possible for us to be to purify, enlighten, comfort, and encourage those connected with us in family relation should be done."[8]

When I received my Ph.D. in psychology, I assumed I knew how to counsel any person with personal or marital problems. I anticipated experience would only sharpen my techniques, but most of what I would practice, I learned from my studies. Was I in for a shock! As I involved myself more and more in counseling I soon discovered the books didn't cover the problems of every client I had sitting in front of me. Time and time again I have gone back to the books to refresh my memory of the things I forgot or look for something I don't remember studying. Slowly I became aware that not every case study is recorded in manuals and books. In moments of painful honesty, I've had to admit I knew very little when it came to understanding human behavior. People and their problems are all different. No two counselees who have come to me have the exact same problem. Each situation had to be handled differently. What worked on one I soon discovered might not work on the next. I probably could write a textbook on every situation I have been involved with. The more I read and study, with every counselee who visits my office, the more I understand no one really understands how people think.

I earnestly desire to help every person who knocks on the door of my office. I have come to the conclusion the best way to help anyone is to lead him or her to the Lord. Once they are at His feet, He takes over and leads, guides, counsels, instructs, and directs. My goal as a Biblical counselor and pastor is to assist an individual or couple to change into Christlikeness. God has pledged Himself to reproduce His Son in each of us. He is the only one that speaks the language of every man, woman, and child. He is the only one who can cure the "sin bug" which has infiltrated every soul on earth. He is the only one who can transform any of us into His likeness.

Below you will find what I believe to be the best formula any pastor or counselor can give in guidance to solving a marital or personal problem.

God says; "And be not conformed to this world: but be ye transformed by the renewing of your mind, that ye may prove what is that good, and acceptable, and perfect, will of God" Romans 12:2. *"It is by the renewing of the heart that the grace of God works to transform the life. No mere external change is sufficient to bring us into harmony with God.* There are many that try to reform by correcting this bad habit or that bad habit, and they hope in this way to become Christians, but they are beginning in the wrong place. *Our first work is in the heart.* The leaven of truth works secretly, silently, steadily to transform the soul. The *natural inclinations* are softened and subdued. New thoughts, new feelings, new motives are implanted. A new standard of character is set up—the life of Christ. The mind is changed; the faculties are aroused to action in new lines. Man is not endowed with new faculties, but the faculties he has are sanctified."[9]

When we are transformed in Christlikeness we start learning a new language, the language of heaven. "We need to frame the promises to God, and hang them up in the chambers of the mind, then we can communicate to others the comfort wherewith we are comforted. *Here we are to learn the language of heaven*, whose inhabitants will be our companions through eternity."[10] "When you catch a glimpse of the goodness of God, *you will have a tongue of wisdom. You will have words to speak in season to those that are weary.* You may never have learned the different languages of this earth, *but God will teach you the language of heaven.*"[11] What is the language of heaven? It is the language of love.

"If I speak in the tongues of men and of angels, but have not love, I am only a resounding gong or a clanging cymbal. If I have the gift of prophecy and can fathom all mysteries and all knowledge, and if I have a faith that can move mountains, but have not love, I am nothing. If I give all I possess to the poor and surrender my body to the flames, but have not love, I gain nothing. Love is patient, love is kind. It does not envy, it does not boast, it is not proud. It is not rude, it is not self-seeking, it is not easily angered, it keeps no record of wrongs. Love does not delight in evil but rejoices with the truth. It always protects, always trusts, always hopes, always perseveres. Love never fails. But where there are prophecies, they will cease; where there are tongues, they will be stilled; where there is knowledge, it will pass away. For we know in part and we prophesy in part, but when perfection comes, the imperfect disappears. When I was a child, I talked like a child, I thought like a child, I reasoned like a child. When I became a man, I put childish ways behind me. Now we see but a poor reflection as in a mirror; then we shall see face to face. Now I know in part; then I shall know fully, even as I am fully known. And now these three remain: faith, hope and love. But the greatest of these is love" 1 Corinthians 13:1–13 NIV.

The language of heaven must be learned today. Because "When He comes He is not to cleanse us of our sins, to remove from us the defects in our characters, or to cure us of the infirmities of our tempers and dispositions... When the Lord comes, those who are holy will be holy still... But those who are unjust, unsanctified, and filthy will remain so forever... We are now in God's workshop. Many of us are rough stones from the quarry. But as we lay hold upon the truth of God, its influence affects us. It elevates us and removes from us every imperfection and sin, of whatever nature.... It is here that this work is to be accomplished for us, here that our bodies and spirits are to be fitted for immortality."[12]

Chapter 13

"God's Pillars for a Happy Marriage"

Recently I became a member of the American Association of Christian Counselors (AACC). This is an organization out of Virginia dedicated to promoting and assisting Christian Counselors. Their goal is to help Christian counselors and psychologists keep up with the latest in counseling. In their third quarterly magazine issue for 1998, the president and editor, Dr. Gary R. Collins, reported on a thought-provoking book, *The Second Coming of the Church* (Word 1998) by George Barna. Here he explains how the book included a chapter entitled *The Unsinkable True Church*. It was written to help its readers think about ways to build healthy and authentic congregations. Barna suggest that unsinkable churches are built on several different pillars. Dr. Collins commences to compare unsinkable churches to unsinkable Christian counseling practices.

This article started me to wondering, might there also be pillars that support unsinkable marriages? I concluded there is; let's look at a few of them.

To begin with, I believe any strong marriage must be built on God's Word. There must be a knowledge of what God expects. Barna reported "most Americans believe they already know the fundamental truths of the Scriptures, our research has discovered that fewer than 10% of American Christians actually possess a biblical worldview." The author also documented that a large percentage of professing Christians have beliefs, which are diametrically opposed to Scripture. It's unfortunate but true anytime there isn't a biblical knowledge of what God has to say on any subject then "most Christians make important decisions on the basis of instinct, emotion, assumptions, past

Chapter 13

experience, external pressure, or chance" (*ibid.*). This made me wonder how many married couples are Biblically illiterate on what the Lord's true plans are for having a happy and complete marriage!

"Marriage was in God's order; it was one of the first institutions which he established. He gave special directions concerning this ordinance, clothing it with sanctity and beauty; but these directions had been forgotten, and marriage had been perverted to minister to passion... The parties do not ask counsel of God, nor have his glory in view. Christianity ought to have a controlling, sanctifying influence upon the marriage relation; but husband and wife are not united by Christian principle; uncontrolled passion lies at the foundation of many of the marriages that are contracted at the present time."[1]

Every Christian must remember that "The Bible presents a perfect standard of character. This sacred book, inspired by God, and written by holy men, *is a perfect guide under all circumstances of life*. It sets forth distinctly the duties of both young and old. If made the guide of life, its teachings will lead the soul upward. It will elevate the mind, improve the character, and give peace and joy to the heart. But many of the young (may I add the old too) have chosen to be their own counselor and guide, and have taken their cases in their own hands. Such need to study more closely the teachings of the Bible. In its pages they will find revealed their duty..."[2]

I find many dedicated Christians today with the full intent on serving God with heart, soul, and mind, lack the basic knowledge on what the Bible teaches on marriage. Too many men feel they can control their wife. "He may even quote texts of Scripture to show that he is the head, and that he must be obeyed in all things. He feels that his wife belongs to him, and that she is subject to his order and dictation. But who gives him the right to thus dictate and condemn? Is it the law of God, which commands him to love God with all his heart, and his neighbor as himself? No; there is no moral or religious defense for such unjust authority. The same Bible that prescribes the duty of the wife, prescribes also the duty of the husband. It says, 'Husbands, love your wives, and be not bitter against them.' The husband is to be kind and affectionate. He is to love his wife as a part of himself, and to cherish her as Christ does his Church."[3] Without knowledge of the Scriptures, many will sink and go down with the boat in never learning how to have a happy marriage. Too many (mostly men, but I have seen a few women do it too) misuse Scripture in trying to make their spouse obey and behave the way they perceive they should. This is morally and ethically wrong. God never sanctioned His Word to be used as a tool against another.

Marriage is so misunderstood in today's modern world. Too many believe marriage is based on love. While it is true that in order to have a truly happy marriage love must be found, but having a happy wedlock goes way past *love*, it takes a solid pillar of *commitment* to each other. Societies today seem to focus on our own individual right to personal happiness. We have the "If it feels good, do it" attitude. We want everything our own way and if we don't get it, then the game "out with the old and in with the new" is played. Through thick and thin, good times as well as bad, God says that marriage is a commitment for life. My neighbor once said to me that he planned to be married for life and so far everything was going as planned.

Learning how to have a happy marriage is a process, which comes to everyone who waits patiently and endures the process. It wasn't too many years ago divorce was unthinkable in some countries and only happened in rare cases. Then the counterculture of the 1960's hit and the world of marriage has never been the same. The traditional marriage system was thrown out the back door. By the 1970's the self-fulfillment movement took place. Self-adulation became the norm with most married couples, and the divorce rate shot up at unbelievable speeds. Today 50% of all marriages end up in the divorce courts. As sad as it is to write, this rate holds true for Christians also.

Many people think that a successful marriage is based on whether both partners are happy. Commitment is thrown away like the old saying; "The baby has been thrown out with the bath water." Many have the thoughts that if my spouse doesn't make me happy then I will just find one that will. Some couples forget, or don't care, what God commanded in His Word about marriage being a lifetime covenant and promise.

You've probably heard; "What you don't know won't hurt you." But this is not true. The devil is trying feverishly to break up every marriage including yours and mine. He knows God's Word unmasks his tactic and game plan. It maps out his strategy and how he plans to increase immorality, pain, sorrow, and heartache in every home. Because he has been so very successful in completely destroying millions of families around the world is why we must read and study what God has to say on marriage being for life. But where should one begin? Does God have a blueprint of how to live happily ever after? Is there a pillar foundation to finding peace and happiness?

Have you ever had a difficult time viewing God's Ten Commandments as a source of finding peace and happiness? Dr. Laura Schlessinger in her book *The Ten Commandments* says; "The Ten Commandments are the first direct communication between a people and God… God's moral laws are still binding. They are the blueprint of God's expectations upon us and His plan for a meaningful, just, loving, holy life. Each of the Ten Commandments asserts a principle…, each principle is a moral focal point for thousands of real life issues, including relating to God, family, our fellows, sex, work, charity, property, speech, and thought."[4] I believe by obeying God's Ten Commandments heavenly tranquility will be experienced in our homes. They are the pillars to finding the Lord's peace, the support that makes a strong marriage. "Those who take Christ at His word, and surrender their souls to His keeping, their lives to His ordering, will find peace and quietude."[5]

As sinful humans, we generally dislike what the law of God says because it goes against our fallen natures. "Because the carnal mind is enmity against God: for it is not subject to the law of God, neither indeed can be." Romans 8:7. We desire to live free and do as we please. But if we truly want to be free and be able to enjoy married life, we must learn to live in complete harmony with God's holy law of liberty. "But whoso looketh into the perfect law of liberty, and continueth therein, he being not a forgetful hearer, but a doer of the work, this man shall be blessed in his deed." James 1:25. God says we are blessed if we stay in harmony and obey His Word.

Only those who obey the laws of harmony can live in perfect happiness. If I cheat on my wife, I will pay the price someday. If I lie to her, it only leads to telling another lie to cover up the first. Remember King David's lies to cover up his sin he committed with Bathsheba? One commandment after another he broke until God sent Nathan the prophet to rebuke David of his sins. When David realized what his lies and dishonesty had caused, his heart was touched, and he penned Palm 51. David asked for forgiveness of his sins and received it, but the damage had been done. When we disobey God's holy law, like David, only hurt, pain, confusion, chaos, and frustration will follow.

In Matthew 5:17 and 18 Jesus says; "Think not that I am come to destroy the law, or the prophets: I am not come to destroy, but to fulfill. For verily I say unto you, Till heaven and earth pass, one jot or one tittle shall in no wise pass from the law, till all be fulfilled. Whosoever therefore shall break one of these least commandments, and shall teach men so, he shall be called the least in the kingdom of heaven: but whosoever shall do and teach them, the same shall be called great in the kingdom of heaven."

In Matthew 22:37–40 Jesus sums up the whole Ten Commandments; "Jesus said unto him, Thou shalt love the Lord thy God with all thy heart, and with all thy soul, and with all thy mind. This is the first and great commandment. And the second is like unto it, Thou shalt love thy neighbour as thyself. On these two commandments hang all the law and the prophets."

Chapter 13

When commenting on God's Holy law, one author wrote; "From the first the great controversy had been upon the law of God. Satan had sought to prove that God was unjust, that His law was faulty, and that the good of the universe required it to be changed. In attacking the law he aimed to overthrow the authority of its Author. In the controversy it was to be shown whether the divine statutes were defective and subject to change, or perfect and immutable."[6]

Lucifer has been attacking God's laws from the beginning. One goal he had was to try and destroy the Sabbath and the marriage ceremony. Both of these institutions God gave to us as a blessing and both have been attacked by the devil time and time again. Satan has tried to teach humans to believe that the Sabbath is no longer binding or has been changed. He has convinced countless millions that living together is better than the marriage commitment. That marriage is not a necessary pillar for having happiness in a home is Satan's message.

Let's compare God's Holy laws to the holy matrimony union of two people becoming one. The Ten Commandments are much more than just "Thou shall nots." Humanly speaking, they sound negative. But when examined with a positive attitude each commandment is a pronouncement on how to live happily ever after. For example, the commandment "Thou shalt not commit adultery" (Exodus 20:14) is not a commandment to keep me from having fun, but to keep me pure and holy.

When Adam and Eve sinned, the world was deprived of peace and happiness. Satan robbed the peace of mind and tranquility that God had placed in mankind's heart. Sin brought confusion and unrest in individual hearts and sadness in the marriage institution. Adam right away blamed his wife for his mistake and Eve blamed the snake, but both were ultimately blaming God. "Adam could neither deny nor excuse his sin; but instead of manifesting penitence, he endeavored to cast the blame upon his wife, and thus upon God Himself. 'The woman whom Thou gavest to be with me, she gave me of the tree, and I did eat....' When the woman was asked, 'What is this that thou hast done?' she answered, 'The serpent beguiled me, and I did eat.' 'Why didst Thou create the serpent? Why didst Thou suffer him to enter Eden?'—these were the questions implied in her excuse for her sin. Thus, like Adam, she charged God with the responsibility of their fall....Instead of humbly confessing their sins, they try to shield themselves by casting the blame upon others, upon circumstances, or upon God—making even His blessings an occasion of murmuring against Him."[7]

God intended that His holy law was to preserve a close and blissful communion between Himself and mankind. If we violate any of His commandments we cause a conflict between Him and us. Loving obedience to God's will only brings peace and happiness to our heart and marriage. "In heaven there is perfect order, perfect obedience, perfect peace and harmony. Those who have had no respect for order or discipline in this life, would have no respect for the order which is observed in heaven. They can never be admitted into heaven, for all worthy of an entrance there will love order and respect discipline. The characters formed in this, will determine the future life. When Christ shall come, he will not change the character of any individual. Precious, probationary time is given to be improved in washing our robes of character, and making them white in the blood of the Lamb."[8]

I believe the fourth commandment is another pillar that supports an unsinkable marriage. It's found in the heart of the Ten Commandments and was given to remind us Who created us. I believe if mankind as a whole had never forgotten God's Sabbath command we would have the happy homes God created in the Garden of Eden. "God saw that a Sabbath was essential for man, even in Paradise. He needed to lay aside his own interests and pursuits for one day of the seven, that he might more fully contemplate the works of God and meditate upon His power and goodness. He needed a Sabbath to remind him more vividly of God and to awaken gratitude because all that he enjoyed and possessed came from the beneficent hand of the Creator."[9]

Psalms 119:1–7 reads; "Blessed are the undefiled in the way, who walk in the law of the LORD. Blessed are they that keep his testimonies, and that seek him with the whole heart. They also do no iniquity: they walk in his ways. Thou hast commanded us to keep thy precepts diligently. O that my ways were directed to keep thy statutes! Then shall I not be ashamed, when I have respect unto all thy commandments." God's people are blessed when they keep all of His holy laws.

"The law of God is as sacred as God Himself. It is a revelation of His will, a transcript of His character, the expression of divine love and wisdom. The harmony of creation depends upon the perfect conformity of all beings, of everything, animate and inanimate, to the law of the Creator. God has ordained laws for the government, not only of living beings, but of all the operations of nature. Everything is under fixed laws, which cannot be disregarded. But while everything in nature is governed by natural laws, man alone, of all that inhabits the earth, is amenable to moral law. To man, the crowning work of creation, God has given power to understand His requirements, to comprehend the justice and beneficence of His law, and its sacred claims upon him; and of man unswerving obedience is required."[10]

God's law is the law of love. It is the solid foundation a marriage of love will be found built on. God's law was given to us to show we are not to quest for self, to dig and build, to toil and spin, but to reveal how to make life bright, joyous, and beautiful. Like the flowers of the field that gladden and brighten our lives by the ministry of love. Heaven will be the eternal home for all happiness and peace of mind. Everyone in heaven will have God's law of peace written in his or her heart. Doesn't it make sense that we should be able to live that same peace and happiness now? God promises us that we can have the peace of heaven today. Our personal, and married life can be a taste of heaven on earth but only if we live our lives according to God's will today.

When we forget God's law, we forget the solid pillar and foundational force that can hold our marriage together. His law is the only force that will bring true happiness and peace. We owe our total allegiance to Him. When we neglect our allegiance to the Lord, we neglect our happiness that can be found in our home. The price that will be paid for such negligence is a marriage that God's love, power, peace, goodness, and happiness will not be found. Any home that has a strong relationship with God will have a strong relationship between husband and wife. Any home that has a strong relationship with their spouse has solid pillars that will keep their marriage healthy and sturdy.

Chapter 14

"Why Do Such Good Looking Ladies Marry Such Ugly Looking Men?"

"Around every family there is a sacred circle that should be kept unbroken. *Within this circle no other person has a right to come.* Let not the husband or the wife permit another to share the confidences that belong solely to themselves."[1] "The fruit of the Spirit is love, joy, peace, longsuffering, kindness, goodness, faithfulness, gentleness, self-control." Galatians 5:22,23 NKJV. "For to be carnally minded is death, but to be spiritually minded is life and peace." Romans 8:6 NKJV.

I've probably used the story below in more counseling sessions than any other example I know on love and complete forgiveness. The story goes like this. There were two men in a bar drinking heavily late one evening when one turned to the other and said; "I bet you a hundred dollars that I have the best wife in the whole city." To this the other drunk said, "No way! I have the best wife in the whole city and here's my hundred dollars. The bet is on. We'll go to your home first, then mine." The two men left the bar and arrived at the first man's home around 2:00 am and came in the front door making all sorts of racket. One drunk thought to himself; "At my home I have to come in the back door and be very quiet." The first drunk yelled upstairs, "Hey, old lady! Get up and come down and make us some breakfast!" To the shock and amazement of the second drunk, the woman did just as she was told. She came down the stairs smiling as she tried to fix her hair back. "Honey," she said, "I'm glad you made it home safely. Who is your friend?" The second man stood there trying to hold his mouth shut. All he could think of was how his wife would be looking for her rolling pin. The first man said to his wife. "We want you to make us some biscuits and gravy, fresh squeezed orange juice, eggs, and oatmeal." The woman smiled and said she would get right on it. The second drunk could not believe what he was seeing and hearing. But he couldn't admit it to his friend or he would lose his hundred dollars.

Soon breakfast was ready and the men started eating. Throughout the whole breakfast, the wife would repeatedly ask if there were anything else they might want. Finally the second man not being able to stand it any longer placed his hundred dollars on the table and said; "You win. Here's your money. My wife would never do any of this. You have to have the best wife in town. But tell me, why is she so kind to you? What is your secret?" To this the first man thought for a moment and finally replied; "I don't know! Honey why are you so kind to me. I mistreat you. I never take you out. I spend all of our extra money down at the bar. I've been so ugly to you. Why do you love me and are so forgiving?" She looked at her husband of twenty years and replied, "Sweetheart, I gave my devotion to you in the sight of God when we were married. The marriage vows we took swore us together for life. I said I would love you through thick and thin. Good as well as bad times. Jesus said I am to love and forgive you no matter what. I have tried to show my love and devotion. A long time ago I realized that I might be the only Jesus you may ever meet. Your happiness here on earth may be the only happiness you will ever receive. This may be the only heaven you will ever know."

Ellen White wrote a letter that sounded much like the story you just read. "God has assigned woman her mission; and if she, in her humble way, yet to the best of her ability, *makes a heaven of her home*, faithfully and lovingly performing her duties to her husband and children, continually seeking to let a holy light shine from her useful, pure, and virtuous life to brighten all around her, she is doing the work left her of the Master, and will hear from His divine lips the words: Well done, good and faithful servant, enter thou into the joy of thy Lord."[2]

Chapter 14

Did the title of this chapter catch your attention? Many of you are probably hoping I will give you the answer to why some good looking ladies marry some of the ugliest looking men you've ever seen. Well, I'm not going to give you the answer to that dilemma — until the end of this chapter. Sorry.

Do you remember your wedding? If you are like most of us you stood there with sweaty palms and cold feet holding the hand of your spouse to be. It was possibly the happiest moment of your life. You had been planning for this day for sometime, and it had finally arrived. Then after the wedding came your honeymoon. The special moment when you got to know your new marriage partner in a totally new light you had never experienced before. It was the moment when you received one of the greatest blessings God gave the human race. No one can fully comprehend why God made us the way He did. The Bible says in Genesis 1:27, "So God created man in his own image, in the image of God created he him; male and female created he them." God created mankind in His image. Not the likeness of a monkey or a horse, but a mirror of Himself. The Bible "clearly set forth the origin of the human race; and the divine record is so plainly stated that there is no occasion for erroneous conclusions. God created man in His own image. Here is no mystery. There is no ground for the supposition that man was evolved by slow degrees of development from the lower forms of animal or vegetable life."[3]

After God said it was not good for man to be alone "God Himself gave Adam a companion. He provided 'an help meet for him'—a helper corresponding to him-one who was fitted to be his companion, and who could be one with him in love and sympathy. Eve was created from a rib taken from the side of Adam, signifying that she was not to control him as the head, nor to be trampled under his feet as an inferior, but to stand by his side as an equal, to be loved and protected by him. A part of man, bone of his bone, and flesh of his flesh, she was his second self, showing the close union and the affectionate attachment that should exist in this relation.

'For no man ever yet hated his own flesh; but nourisheth and cherisheth it.' Ephesians 5:29. 'Therefore shall a man leave his father and his mother, and shall cleave unto his wife; and they shall be one.'"[4]

Shortly after the shortest engagement in history the Lord performed the first wedding. Thus the institution of marriage has the Creator of the universe as its originator. "Marriage is honorable" Hebrews 13:4; it was one of the first gifts of God to man, and it is one of the two institutions that, after the fall, Adam brought with him beyond the gates of Paradise. According to Genesis 1:26–31, the human race was created on the sixth day of creation. In was in the garden before sin that God instructed Adam and Eve to be "Fruitful and Multiply" (v:28). When God gave humans the ability to procreate He did so as a crowing display of His divine power and image. The gift of sexual intimacy is only within the human race. Jesus Himself declared that the angelic race neither marries nor is given in marriage. "For in the resurrection they neither marry, nor are given in marriage, but are as the angels of God in heaven." Matthew 22.30. Since God gave only humanity the ability to recreate in His image, Satan is so diabolically enraged to destroy the beauty of this gift. Neither a male nor female alone is created in the image of God. It takes both man and woman to form the complete union that reveals God's image. God said "For this cause shall a man leave father and mother, and shall cleave to his wife: and they twain shall be one flesh? Wherefore they are no more twain, but one flesh. What therefore God hath joined together let not man put asunder." Matthew 19.5–6. This one flesh sexual intimacy was given as a gift for a man and woman to enjoy only in the confines of marriage. It is a blessing that is not to be shared with anyone outside the wall of marriage. But "it was Satan's studied effort to pervert the marriage institution, to weaken its obligations and lessen its sacredness; for in no surer way could he deface the image of God in man and open the door to misery and vice."[5]

Chapter 14

At this point of our journey I would like to get very candid with you in an area that not many Christians like to discuss. A section of marriage some, I have discovered, wish was not part of the package when a couple is united in marriage. It would not be fair to many wedded pairs seeking a happy home if this section wasn't covered. The true facts are that for any marriage to be happy there must be an understanding in all zones of marriage, even the forbidden zone of sex. I've had too many couples in my office with the same difficult dilemma to not cover this portion of our campaign of learning how to live happily ever after.

As I stated in the pervious chapter, I can't help but wonder how many married couples really understand the Bible principles of having a happy and fulfilling marriage? Recently I discovered that understanding a person can be simple, or it can be very confusing. It really all depends on how a person views different matters. Some subjects a person can discuss without thinking twice while other subjects can leave a person feeling uncomfortable and uneasy. Take discussing the "facts of life" for example. For many it's probably the most uncomfortable subject there is to discuss, especially with our children. It's sad but true that many children today are taught that the "facts of life" are not to be discussed or mentioned. Some children are lead to believe that sex is dirty. It's something they *have to do* after they're married but that they would hate it. If sex is dirty then God gave mankind something sinful in the Garden of Eden. But this is not the case. All of God's gifts to humanity are pure and holy. Thoughts of sex being immoral have hurt many new marriages. Many couples on their honeymoon night have inaccurate preconceived ideas about having any sort of intimate relationship with their new spouse. They don't know what to do, how to act or behave. Each of us must understand that sex is neither dirty nor sinful. It's a beautiful gift from God and was given to mankind to enjoy. It is a gift like no other gift. If sex is sinful, why did God make it feel so good? Sin didn't cause us to have this feeling we experience during sexual intercourse. If anything, sin has taken away some of the enjoyment. Sex in the beginning may have been much more enjoyable than it is today. Because Satan has set out to destroy everything God created, he has perverted sex outside of marriage that has caused some to believe it is sinful even in marriage.

I have counseled with many (mostly women) who have the preconceived idea that enjoying themselves during intercourse is sinful and should be avoided. They associate sex as being dirty and that a "good, decent" Christian woman should never enjoy an emotional closeness with their husband. They feel that God looks disapprovingly on two people having fun together in the bedroom. I often ask where they got ideas like these? The answer is almost always the same; "My mother." The phrase "If it feels good, do it" has little meaning to them. Most are taught that "if it feels good, then it must be sinful." I wonder how God must feel about people that believe that way? People have made something that God pronounced good, bad. I believe it must make Him sad. As sad as it does when He sees people perverting sexual moments. There are boundaries on sex even within the bounds of marriage. Making one's partner do something in the way of sex when they feel it is totally improper is wrong just as sex outside of marriage is. We must never forget that God made us with every body part we have, internal as well as external. God saw that everything He made was "very good." The only thing God saw that wasn't good was for man to be alone. "And the LORD God said, It is not good that the man should be alone; I will make him an help meet for him." Genesis 2:18. Our attitude toward sex will have a major response on how well anyone will enjoy the togetherness with his or her mate. If a change of attitude is needed, then it must be changed. Do not try to change your spouse's attitude, for this will never work. You can only change your attitude.

After any couple is married they have the opportunity to make another creature like him or herself. This was the Lord's plan before sin ever entered into this world. This same process of repopulating the world is to continue until He returns. God enjoys watching babies grow up just like we do. He also expects us as parents to raise our children to love and obey Him by keeping His laws and continue the same process as they grow up.

God took time to explain the "facts of life" to Adam and Eve there in the garden. He told them to be "fruitful and multiply." He explained His love and how and why they were to obey Him. As God explained to Adam and Eve how to have an intimate relationship with each other He took one step more and explained how He desires to have an intimate relationship with them too. God felt it necessary to elucidate how He planned to get close to them and have that personal relationship. A relationship that no one else would be involved in. A special time of closeness like when two become one. I believe He does the same today. In His Word we find that He still desires to be with mankind. A special intimate closeness that no one else is to be involved in. As I stated in the previous chapter, I believe this is where the Sabbath comes in. It is a time set aside to meet God and communicate our true inner feelings. I pray that just as you take time for your mate you will take time for God too. For no home will ever be happy if Jesus isn't found there.

In the book *The Family*,[6] the authors implied that marriage is not "legalism," but it is "idealism." It is caring for the needs of their spouse. It is a balance of give and take. This is in all areas of marriage, including the bedroom. The Bible says that sex is to be enjoyed by *both* married partners. It is an expression of our love for one another. Scripture upholds that mutual pleasure between each other is a must. 1 Corinthians 7:3–5 indicates that our bodies are for one another to enjoy. It is the ultimate expression of our love to the other. But if sex is viewed only as the right to personal pleasure or as a duty, then the marriage will suffer and love will slowly fade out of sight. The Bible teaches that Christians must not deprive one another of the intimate privileges of marriage, except for a limited time, under special circumstances and by mutual consent.

Being close and having physical contact is absolutely essential for having happiness. True happiness only comes from being close enough to each other that you can feel their true inner desires; knowing what pleases and what doesn't. Keeping oneself isolated from the other never brings anything but grief and sadness. Being close doesn't always mean you have to have sexual intercourse. Learning to laugh and enjoy each other by playing around has always brought true happiness in any home. Being overly serious *all* the time can be dangerous. In happy homes you will find a time to be serious and time to play, "a time to weep and a time to laugh, a time to mourn and a time to dance, a time to scatter stones and a time to gather them, a time to embrace and a time to refrain." Ecclesiastes 3:4,5. Overdoing and underdoing anything can become a grave matter. It can bury a marriage if not careful. It doesn't matter what temperament you are, if you are serious *all* the time it will only weaken your marriage and the ability to love and respect one another. Even Jesus took time to play. "Jesus loved the children. He remembered that he was once a child, and his benevolent countenance won the affections of the little ones. They loved to play around him, and to stroke that loving face with their innocent hands."[7]

We are also counseled that a "relaxation from study, occupations pursued in the open air, and affording exercise for the whole body, are the most beneficial."[8] "It is right that we should choose places for seasons of relaxation and recreation."[9] It is ok with the Lord to take time to play and relax.

In the beginning, God made man and woman different in the way they see and enjoy sex. For men sex is not a complicated matter. He only has to look at his wife and can desire her. The woman's desire for her husband is different. For her sex is more involved with relationships, feelings, and presentation. She needs time and it starts in the morning. A man doesn't need a candlelight dinner to get him in the mood. A simple thought of the light switch being turned off will turn him on. The wife on the other hand desires to be cooed and appreciated before her husband will make it to first base with her. She needs to be able to communicate her feelings before she can open her heart and really enjoy the emotional closeness with her husband. She needs to know that her man loves her for who she is, not what he will get.

There is so much involved such as our biology, gender, feelings, behaviors, attitudes, values, and temperaments that make up a sexual person. What causes one gender to respond sexually to the opposite gender? What makes one desire to turn and look at the opposite sex when one should pass us by? There can only be one answer; God made us to desire the opposite sex. He also gave us guidelines on how and when to respond. Sex before marriage was never permitted by God. Satan has taken this God given gift and has perverted it to the point that many misunderstand its full meaning. We must remember that sin comes from the misuse of sex, not from its mere existence. God fully understands and recognizes that the sexual drive in humans is a very powerful element of our total being, a forceful drive. A drive in most human beings that needs to be met and fulfilled.

I'm sure all of us are aware and familiar with the women's monthly curse. This is when a woman metamorphoses from Mrs. ever-so-nice, Dr. Jekell, into Mrs. ever-so dreaded, Mrs. Hyde. The bloating and swelling starts. Temper rises. The week, which seems like it will go for eternity has begun. What so few people (especially women) realize is that many men are cursed too. Most men are cursed with the desire, need, and want of sex anytime or place!

WAIT! Don't close the book yet ladies. You made it this far. Please let me explain. We probably all know how a male animal reacts whenever a female animal is in heat. It seems a fence cannot be built high enough to hold a dog in when he smells a female dog in heat. A tomcat roams around the house meowing and howling. If we could understand his language he would probably be saying, "Let me out, I have business to take care of."

For some reason most males, whether they are human or animals want the act and satisfaction that comes with sex. I believe this is possibly one reason why some men can have a one night stand with no relationship involved, where as the woman wants and needs a relationship tie that lasts. Women need to know they are loved and appreciated while most men just want the act and satisfaction. Whether you are a male or female I realize this is probably difficult for you to understand about the opposite sex, but the fact is that in most cases it is true. "I'm a firm believer that women give sex to get love and men give love to get sex."

Did you notice I said "most males," not "all males" have a desire for sex anytime or place? During my research I have uncovered the fact that some phlegmatic men have no desire for sexual intercourse. I've had several women come to me with a confused hurt that something must be wrong with them. It appears that their husbands almost never have a desire for lovemaking. A few women have enlightened me that on their honeymoon their husband had no desire to hold them or for sex. The only common thread I could find was that their husbands were all phlegmatics. During a seminar once I made the above statement and had a woman bring her phlegmatic husband up to me and said, (in front of him) that I was so right. When I looked toward him to see what he had to say all he did was shrug his shoulders and say; "It's only sex."

Men that want a one night stand remind me of the "Once saved always saved" theory. Some Christians want a one-time experience with Jesus then walk away. Their need and desire has been satisfied and met. They feel no need of a continuing relationship with Jesus. But just like the theory of "Once saved always saved" is wrong, so are one night stands.

This brings me to another thought. Women, never underestimate the ego of a man. The issue is not whether ego is right or wrong, nor whether it is Scriptural. It doesn't matter whether you agree with me or not. In a man's subliminal self-image of himself you will find a man's ego is huge, especially when it comes to the bedroom scenario. Most men feel, believe, and preach that he is the world's best there is in the bedroom. He believes he could write a book on the art of lovemaking. When his ego is degraded in his

Chapter 14

sexual ability, it will destroy his love. Pastor Robert. L. Russell gave the story once while conducting a wedding ceremonial about Jack Dempsey's wife. It seemed she was asked how she enjoyed being married to a boxer. To this she quickly replied; "I didn't marry a boxer. I married a champion!" Make your husband feel like a champion, and he will act like one. Communication plays a huge role in the whole meshing process. Learning to effectively communicate whether verbal or nonverbal can enhance the process of becoming together as one. Sex was made by God for two people after they are married to become one and enjoy each other in a totally different and unique way. Mankind could have never thought up the beautiful design of sex. Only a loving God that wanted to give His children everything could have thought up the sexual intimacy of two becoming one. But sexual abuse will only destroy love, it never intensifies it. Your marriage license does not give you the liberty to defile your mate's trust. The Bible is clear that we are to have a temperate sex life. "The husband should fulfill his marital duty to his wife, and likewise the wife to her husband. The wife's body does not belong to her alone but also to her husband. In the same way, the husband's body does not belong to him alone but also to his wife. Do not deprive each other except by mutual consent and for a time, so that you may devote yourselves to prayer. Then come together again so that Satan will not tempt you because of your lack of self-control. I say this as a concession, not as a command. I wish that all men were as I am. But each man has his own gift from God; one has this gift, another has that." 1 Corinthians 7:3–7 NIV.

I once counseled with a man who had tried to explain his feelings about sex to his wife. He felt she needed to know how much he enjoyed and needed sex almost every night. He enjoyed sex and couldn't (or wouldn't) understand why his wife didn't enjoy sex as much as he did. He read self-learn books on how to improve his sex life and please his mate. He came to see me after reading a book on the gift of sex. This book was totally different than what he had been reading. In it he discovered that a husband rapes his wife if he demands or requires sex from her. This shocked and made him nauseated to his stomach. When he talked it over with his wife about what he had read, he came to understand that his wife had been unwillingly giving in to him each week. Because of her desire to serve God, she gave in to his wishes even though he was repulsive to her. The repugnant feeling inside her had been going on since shortly after they were married. By the time he came to see me he was almost to the point of suicide or leaving his wife. This Christian man could not believe what he had been doing to his loving wife. For weeks he could not look at her in the face. But over time, counseling, and much prayer, he was able to forgive himself. Today, their marriage is stronger than ever. He no longer demands or requires sex from his wife. They meet together on mutual grounds when both are in the mood.

Men, if you are demanding or requiring sex from your wife when she is not in the mood, then you too are raping her. Sex is to be enjoyed by both partners. It is a special time, a holy time that God blessed to be shared. Learn to communicate your feelings to each other. Listen to the other as they talk. Learn to speak and understand each other's language. If you can't understand the others inner feelings, then accept the fact that this is the way they feel. For no truly happy spouse would want to withhold his or her love from the other. When the core of one's being is shared and understood, or accepted, you will find that sharing their love will be too.

I had another couple come to me for marriage counseling. It seemed he wanted sex all the time. Anytime and place. If they were driving and the mood hit him, he would simply find some side road and pull over, even if the kids were in the back seat. Thankfully he would wait until they were asleep. He constantly would talk her into lovemaking when she didn't want to. If she said she was not in the mood, he would force himself on her. Men, I will say it again, this is called rape! No one has the right to abuse his or her spouse in any shape, form, or fashion. God never gave anyone that authority! By the time she came to me, she was in a very emotional state. His degrading, twisted, and intemperate sex acts had destroyed her love and respect for him completely. "No man can truly love his wife if she will patiently submit to become his slave, and minister to his degraded passions... When the wife yields her body and mind to the control of her husband, being passive to his will in all things, sacrificing her conscience, her dignity, and even her identity, she loses the opportunity of exerting that mighty influence for good which she should possess to elevate her husband. She could soften his stern nature, and her sanctifying influence could be exerted in a manner to refine, purify, and lead him to strive earnestly to govern his passions, and be more spiritually minded, that they might be partakers together of the divine nature, having escaped the corruption that is in the world through lust. The power of influence can be great to lead the mind to high and noble themes, above the low, sensual indulgences which the heart unrenewed by grace naturally seeks. If the wife feels that she must, in order to please her husband, come down to his standard, when animal passion is the principal basis of his love, controlling his actions, she displeases God; for she fails to exert a sanctifying influence upon her husband. If she feels that she must submit to the animal passions of her husband without a word of remonstrance, she does not understand her duty to him, nor to her God. Sexual excess will effectually destroy a love for devotional exercises, will take from the brain the substance needed to nourish the system, and will most effectually exhaust the vitality. No woman should aid her husband in this work of self-destruction. She will not do it if she is enlightened, and truly loves her husband."[10]

Picking the right time to talk is very important. Any fool can speak or act at the wrong time. Being discreet in knowing when and what to say makes all the difference on how the outcome will end up. The Bible tells us in Ecclesiastes 3:5–7 that there is a time for everything in life. "A time to embrace, and a time to refrain from embracing; A time to get, and a time to lose; a time to keep, and a time to cast away; A time to rend, and a time to sew; a time to keep silence, and a time to speak." Knowing when to speak to your mate about certain things that matter to you is very important to understand. Talking about something that bothers the wife when he is watching a ball game is bad timing. Expressing the needs or wants to the wife when she has a headache or is cleaning the house usually gets nowhere. Knowing proper timing when to speak about things in any marriage will make all the difference in the world on the outcome. That's like knowing when to fly a kite.

I grew up in sunny and windy west Texas. As a young boy I liked to fly kites. My favorite was and still is the box kite. I loved standing my kite up on its end and with just one pull, she would be up there soaring with the eagles. But one day I learned the hard way about trying to fly my kite during a west Texas sand storm. I figured she would fly better when the wind was stronger. Wrong! She went up and came down with a huge crash! And that is what will happen if you try to speak about matters in your marriage at the wrong time. It doesn't matter how complex and difficult your marriage may be at this time, God can unravel and repair it. No matter how difficult your spouse may be to understand, God can give you strength to accept them for who they are. We must accept that there is nothing too difficult for God to do through and for us if we will allow Him to. We can commit our life and marriage to Him with absolute confidence that He will work everything out for our best. God can make the best out of the worst of marriages.

Ok, it's time for the answer of "Why good-looking ladies marry such ugly looking men." Looks have nothing to do with it. Marriage is based on a love relationship. And it's on that same basis, that same love relationship that God gave us marriage. If your marriage to your spouse is based on looks, then your marriage is in big trouble.

Much education is needed on both the husband and wife's part in order to truly understand and enjoy each other. When one doesn't care if they please the other, then problems will arise and there will never be a really happy home. We must take time to educate ourselves in this area. Learning what is pleasing to your spouse will only enhance this great gift that God gave mankind in the beginning. A gift that will last as long as we are on this earth. How we use this gift is up to us. We can use it to His glory or we can abuse it. If we truly love God, if we truly love our mates, then we will enjoy sex only the way God wanted it to be enjoyed. Sex will never wear out like other gifts we receive. Not unless we let it wear out. It only gets better as it becomes more enjoyed.

Chapter 15

"The Storms of Marriage" [1]

"'If I ascend up into heaven, thou art there: if I make my bed in hell, behold, thou art there. If I take the wings of the morning, and dwell in the uttermost parts of the sea; Even there shall thy hand lead me, and thy right hand shall hold me. If I say, Surely the darkness shall cover me; even the night shall be light about me. Yea, the darkness hideth not from thee; but the night shineth as the day: the darkness and the light are both alike to thee. For thou hast possessed my reins' Psalms 139:8–13. From age to age the Lord has made known the manner of His working. When a crisis has come, He has revealed Himself, and has interposed to hinder the working out of Satan's plans. With nations, with families, and with individuals, He has often permitted matters to come to a crisis, that His interference might become marked. Then He has made manifest that there is a God in Israel who will maintain His law and vindicate His people."[2]

I read a story about a man that hated his ex-wife. He hated her much more after the divorce was final. It was one of those bad divorces. She had cheated on him and yet somehow she ended up with the kids, house, car, and the family dog. She got everything. She had lied to the judge about how bad a husband and father he was. She also explained that he never listened to her. This caused him to be very angry and wanted to get even. One night an angel appeared to him in a dream. In his dream the angel said; "I will give you anything you request, but know this, your ex-wife will receive twice as much as I give you. You can be rich. You can be healthy. You can be anything or anyone you like, but your ex-wife will receive twice as much. What is

Chapter 15

your desire?" The man thought long and hard and finally said; "Strike me blind in one eye!"

Have you read in the news lately about any storm activity? Ever heard of the El Nino weather system? At the time of this writing El Nino has passed over and La Nina is on the scene. Many claim it will be worse than El Nino. It's not uncommon that whenever a storm strikes a Christian's home, and it is destroyed or damaged, we often ask; "Why Lord? Why?" We want to know why bad things happen to good people? We wonder if God cares about His children anymore? We could understand why bad things happen to those who do not follow God's Laws. That would make sense, but do bad things have to happen to the good people?

Can you think of any Bible stories where something really bad happened to someone really good? Probably the first story that pops in your mind is the story of Job. In Job 1:8, God calls Job "A perfect and upright man, one that fears God and shuns evil." NKJV. I believe during this time of trial for Job, he must have felt like he was going through some sort of bad storm. How about Joseph? Doesn't the Bible tell us in Genesis 39:2 that "The Lord was with Joseph?" Yet his brothers sold him into slavery. His boss's wife falsely accused him and he was thrown into prison for three years because of it. I believe he also must have felt he was walking through a mighty strong storm. Over and over our Bible is full of stories about perfectly good people that stayed true to their faith, and yet many of them went through some strong storms sometime in their life.

In this chapter I hope to share with you some principles that I believe will help you make sense of why marriages sometimes go through storms of life. I also want to cover the subject of forgiving others who have hurt us.

My wife and I experienced some bad blizzards while living in Iowa. We've seen the results of ice storms in Mississippi. I've lived through west Texas sandstorms and east Texas floods. America, along with other countries just experienced what some are calling the hurricane of the century, Mitch. Thousands were killed because of the floods and mudslides. People have been asking; "Why Lord, Why?" Yes, the storms of Mother Nature are raging all around us. But what about the storms of marriage?

The Bible speaks about many storms. One is found in Matthew 14:22: "And straightway Jesus constrained his disciples to get into a ship, and to go before him unto the other side, while he sent the multitudes away." The story here picks up just after the miracle of the feeding the five thousand. The Bible tells us that just after the completion of that event Jesus told His disciples to "Get into the boat and go to the other side." The implication here is that Jesus was going to meet up with them on the other side later. But John 6:16 says that it wasn't until evening that the disciples did what the Lord told them to do. They waited for a while because they were hoping that Jesus would come with them. When they saw that darkness was coming, John 6:17 says it was then that they "entered into a ship, and went over the sea toward Capernaum," but on their way they ran into a violent storm.

They were doing exactly what Jesus told them to do. They were exactly where the Lord wanted them to be and yet a terrible storm blew up.

Have you ever noticed that as humans it seems that whenever we face difficulties in life we try to find out what is causing the storm we are facing? We have the tendency to want to question God on why we have to go through any trials. We quickly stop to think if we had done something sinful or bad. We run down the list of commandments checking each one to see if we have broken one lately. For some unknown reason most of us have been conditioned to associate difficulties with disobedience. We often feel that if we live as a Christian should live, obey the Ten Commandments, keep the health laws, watch how we observe the Sabbath; we automatically receive a by-pass around the storms of life. Obstacles in the road are moved out of our way. We feel that difficulty and trials are for the "bad people," not us "saints." We hoped that when we accepted Christ we would be exempt from trials and tribulations in our life now and forever more. But the facts are, it doesn't matter if you are obedient or disobedient, just living in a sinful world can place you in the midst of a storm. Although the Scriptures don't cover much about Bible characters' home life, I can't help but believe that they too had disagreements with their spouse at times. Job's wife told him to curse God and die. Hosea had to go and buy his wife Gomer from the slave's auction. Adam and Eve didn't see eye to eye on eating the forbidden fruit.

In today's modern world if you're unfaithful to your spouse you might catch AIDS or some other dreaded disease. If you smoke you stand a good chance of developing lung cancer. Those who drink alcohol face developing liver disease or killing themselves (or others) while driving. If you eat the wrong kind of food there are all sorts of diseases that might be knocking at your door. But these verses in Matthew 14:22–33 imply that we can do exactly what God wants us to do, we can be exactly where God wants us to be, and still find ourselves in the center stage of a violent storm.

Mark 6:48 says that Jesus watched this small little boat from the shoreline. John 6:19 says that they were about three miles out to sea and yet Jesus could see these fear-stricken men battling with the strong winds and high waves. *The Desire of Ages*, page 381 says that; "Jesus had not forgotten them. The Watcher on the shore saw those fear-stricken men battling with the tempest. Not for a moment did He lose sight of His disciples. With deepest solicitude His eyes followed the storm-tossed boat with its precious burden; for these men were to be the light of the world. As a mother in tender love watches her child, so the compassionate Master watched His disciples."

Do you want to know what Jesus does for us when a storm, trial, or problem brews up? Isaiah 43:2–3 says that; "When thou passest through the waters, I will be with thee;… when thou walkest through the fire, thou shalt not be burned;…For I am the LORD thy God,… thy Saviour…" The Lord will meet us in the middle of any earthly storm. He is with us when our life seems to be torn apart with the affairs of life.

Some of us have gotten so caught up in the storms of our marriage that we have lost sight of Jesus. We don't recognize that maybe God is trying to speak to us through the tempest. I discovered long ago that from time to time God might produce turbulence in order to speak to us in such a way that we'll hear Him when we don't hear Him in the calm. The pen of inspiration wrote about the disciples during this stormy night. "They were in the midst of troubled waters. Their thoughts were stormy and unreasonable, and *the Lord gave them something* else to afflict their souls and occupy their minds. God *often* does this when men create burdens and troubles for themselves."[3]

"*Often*," and that's the word she used, God has to send us a wake up call. I've always been curious why it is when things are going well in our life we have the tendency not to spend a great deal of time down on our knees. But let the chips fall, let something go wrong in our life, and we want to make a quick appointment date with God.

Well, there are times when God calls and makes an appointment date with us. Have you ever noticed that when the storms in our marriage are raging, we're down on our knees praying making vows that we know we will have a hard time keeping. Why do we do this? The answer is simple. It's because the storm has gotten our attention. And from time to time God has to get our attention.

Any marriage will have its ups and downs. There will be days of exaltation and days of despair. The weather is mixed with sunshine and shadows from clouds. There are valleys to cross and mountains to climb. Sailing smooth seas one day and raging wind storms the next. But through it all, in spite of all the bad days, there are good days just around the corner, across the valley, and after the rain stops. King Solomon once wrote; "For lo, the winter is past, the rain is over and gone. The flowers appear on the earth" *Song of Solomon* 2:11,12.

Chapter 15

It's hard to believe that Paul, whom I believe was a strong choleric, could write one of the most beautiful chapters found in the New Testament on love and forgiveness, 1 Corinthians 13; *"The love chapter."* Here he released his true inner feelings on how he felt love should be expressed. He laid it on the line that true love is based on true forgiveness.

Have you ever considered that sometimes our feelings against someone else can cause an emotional and spiritual cancer that can and will destroy any relationship. Hate, depression, stress, and anger are like acid. If left long enough it will eat through its container.

One huge misconception most Christians have is the belief that the Bible and the Spirit of Prophecy claim we are to forgive and *forget* any hurt that has come our way. How can we *forget* the hurt someone has done to us? Do we have a delete key like computers that will erase or blot out the hurt someone caused us? As Christians we often talk about that if we can't *forget* the hurt that has come our way then God will not forget and forgive us of our sins. In all my immense amount of research on forgetting hurt I could not find one verse or quote that says we are to forgive and *forget* a wrong that was done to us. Sure I could find many verses about forgiveness. "Judge not, and ye shall not be judged: condemn not, and ye shall not be condemned: forgive, and ye shall be forgiven." Luke 6:37. "For if ye forgive men their trespasses, your heavenly Father will also forgive you: But if ye forgive not men their trespasses, neither will your Father forgive your trespasses." Matthew 6:14,15. "Then came Peter to him, and said, Lord, how oft shall my brother sin against me, and I forgive him? till seven times? Jesus saith unto him, I say not unto thee, Until seven times: but, Until seventy times seven." Matthew 18:21,22. "Take heed to yourselves: If thy brother trespass against thee, rebuke him; and if he repent, forgive him." Luke 17:3. "One man is never to say to another, 'When I see that you have reformed, then I will forgive you.' This is not God's plan. This is in accordance with the promptings of human nature. By showing that you do not desire fellowship with your brother, you not only hurt his soul and your own, but you also wound and bruise the heart of Christ."[4] Verse after verse, quote after quote on forgiveness but I could find nothing on having to *forget* the pain in order to receive forgiveness from God. Now before anyone misconstrues what I just said, let me say that we should never harbor or foster the hurt. We must ask God to help us forgive and *forget* the wrong.

A real born-again Christian believes in forgiveness because he or she will include in their prayers; "Lord, Forgive us our trespasses." But how often do we add: "As we forgive those that have trespassed against us?" Forgiveness is a two way street. We must forgive others before we will receive forgiveness. To the ones that won't forgive, God says He can't forgive. I have found that many cholerics, unless born again, seem to have the hardest problem of forgiving someone. Melancholies are like elephants; they can't seem to forget a hurt. Of all temperaments, it appears that the sanguine has the easiest ability to forgive and forget. Mainly because they can't remember anything from one day to the next. Phlegmatics usually won't let things bother them. Often they just shrug their shoulders and say; "Oh well, live and learn." Even though the phlegmatic and sanguine seem to have an easier bout with hurt, the truth is that hurt is real to all temperaments, and each handles pain and hurt differently.

In *Christ Object Lesson*, page 251 we find that *"We are not forgiven because we forgive, but as we forgive. The ground of all forgiveness is found in the unmerited love of God, but by our attitude toward others we show whether we have made that love our own. Wherefore Christ says, 'With what judgment ye judge, ye shall be judged; and with what measure ye mete, it shall be measured to you again.'"* Matthew 7:2. (*Emphasis added*) True forgiveness is both incoming and outgoing. "Therefore all things whatsoever ye would that men should do to you, do ye even so to them." Matthew 7:12. An unforgiving Christian is nothing more than an oxymoron.

Chapter 15

Learning to apologize is also an art that takes prayer, time, and practice. A person should keep trying different ways to apologize until they discover what works with their spouse. Picking the right time is usually the best thing to learn first. Find a place and time where you know you will not be distracted or disturbed and the two of you can sit down to discuss the problem. As a rule while riding in a car is usually a good time. That is unless you have a spouse that gets physical if the two of you disagree and cannot come to a happy medium. I counseled a man once that, if a disagreement broke out while he was driving their car, his wife would start pulling his hair. Believe me, this is not healthy or safe.

Another good rule is not to blame the other for whatever has happened. Pastor Morris Venden gives the story about a seminar that was being held where the instructor asked this question. "Who is supposed to initiate and say they are sorry first when there has been a problem or argument: the one who was in the right or the one who was in the wrong?" Almost every answer was "Of course, the one in the wrong." The instructor replied, "No, that's wrong! The one in the wrong is too emotionally disturbed to be able to admit they are wrong at that moment. It must always be the one in the right to take the first steps in saying, 'I'm sorry. Forgive me.'" You realize that this could cause another problem if both parties think they are in the right and try to initiate first the apology. If not careful, another even more heated debate can commence. But when that principle is applied to God, it is always true. He took the first steps in the garden when our first parents transgressed. He is the same God that stands at your door and knocks today asking to come in and have supper with you. "Behold, I stand at the door, and knock: if any man hear my voice, and open the door, I will come in to him, and will sup with him, and he with me." Revelation 3:20.

I don't know why it is, but almost everyone has the natural tendency to hurt and disappoint the one they love the most. Many married persons are much more out to hurt their spouse, children, parents, or friends before they would hurt a perfect stranger. What I've uncovered and found truly sad is that most people hurt the One they should love supremely above all others. As Christians we should love Christ above everyone and everything, yet He is the very One we disappoint the most in the end. For every time we hurt anyone else, we hurt Him too. What we say and how we say it to our spouse, children, family, and friends should be said the same as we would say it to Jesus.

It is impossible to have any kind of a happy marriage while holding any bad feelings about being married. Trying to love someone while being lukewarm to him or her will never cut it. In fact God is against lukewarmness. "I know thy works, that thou art neither cold nor hot: I would thou wert cold or hot. So then because thou art lukewarm, and neither cold nor hot, I will spew thee out of my mouth" Revelation 3:15–16. It will never be of any benefit to a marriage to bow in prayer on mocking knees, a forked tongue, and with an argumentative heart asking God to bless your marriage while holding a grudge.

Two words that work miracles yet are difficult to say are: "I'm sorry." Why is that? Another three words that can bring happiness to any home are: "I love you." If we would learn to speak both of these lines often, naturally, and sincerely, our marriages will grow and grow with each passing day. Speak them face to face with each other. There are times that love notes could be written. But there's something about looking into each other's eyes and feeling the love that sparks behind the sincere words you're sorry that can make all the difference in the world.

Looking at each other's face can create warmth that distance will not produce. Understanding each other grows love. Tolerance becomes more tolerant. The little differences that have brought you to the point of talking begin to recoil and withdraw. The Bible says; "Come, let us look one another in the face" 2 Kings 14:8. Face to face connects the bond you once had and helps heal the pain and hurt.

Chapter 15

Keep in mind that we don't always receive exactly what we pray for. You remember the disciples wanted Jesus to let the crowd crown Him as king and attack the city of Herod. But what did they get? Just the opposite. The disciples wanted Jesus to let the 5,000 men plus women and children go home to eat. But what did they get? Just the opposite. The disciples wanted Jesus to cross the sea with them. But what did they get? Just the opposite. Moses wanted God to find someone else to lead the His people out of Egypt. But what did he get? Just the opposite. God may give us just the opposite of what we pray for. Why? Because He knows best. When we trust Him we have nothing to worry about.

I've been told that the divorce rate in America is higher than any other country in the world. 50% of all marriages in America end up in the divorce courts. Most marriages only last seven years or less. The average is only two to three years. This is sad when so many could work out their problems if they really wanted to. In today's world many want to throw away their marriage and start over with a new spouse. Newly formed marriages are as common as buying a new car. You buy a new car and drive it for a while. If it suits your needs you'll keep it for a while. If not, then trade it in for a newer and better model. I wonder how sad divorce makes God? It must really hurt Him when He looks down upon this world and sees the institution He created becoming nothing more than a joke with so many.

There is no one single cause for divorce. Each spouse has his or her reason for wanting a divorce even if the reason doesn't make sense to the other. They were hurt or disappointed to the point that they want out of the marriage. Divorce causes pain that will take some time to get over. A lot depends on the person(s) involved. It has been said that divorce is worse than death because at death the relationship ends, but with a divorce, although the marriage is over, a relationship of some kind continues. It's not the same kind of relationship, but nevertheless it is a relationship that will continue as long as you live especially when children are involved. Divorce also has a terrible effect on the children.

A Powerful Marriage

They suffer for the rest of their lives. In fact there is evidence that children of divorced parents are likely to experience a divorce themselves.

With all the changes that have taken place in this modern world, it is little wonder that the average family can survive. Very few families hold up true Biblical views and morals anymore. God hasn't changed His ideal family principles and standards, but it seems that modern man has walked away from everything God had planned in the beginning for His perfect world. Sin has taken its toll on not only individuals, but also the entire family structure. And it is getting worse with each passing day. Where will it end? The only answer is we as families have got to get back to God's Word and His original plan for mankind. Not until we do this will life become normal for families. It will not be easy, but it can be done with God's help.

The Scripture says in Mark 11:25–26; "And when ye stand praying, forgive, if ye have ought against any: that your Father also which is in heaven may forgive you your trespasses. But if ye do not forgive, neither will your Father which is in heaven forgive your trespasses." Listen to the Seventh-day Adventist Commentary on this verse: "He who is unwilling to forgive others does not deserve to be forgiven. To extend forgiveness to him would be to condone his own unforgiving spirit. To expect of others what one is unwilling to do himself is the very essence of selfishness and sin. God's unwillingness to forgive one who harbors an unforgiving spirit is based on the need of the unforgiving person to overcome a basic character defect. God could not forgive such a person and at the same time be true to His own righteous character. Only when we are right with our fellow men can we be right with God."[5] The way we Christians treat others is the acid test of how real our religion is. "Our attitude toward our fellow men (*our spouse*) is an infallible index of our attitude toward God."[6]

Don't worry if you don't succeed at having a happy home right off. Remember that the oak tree began as an acorn and the rainbow as a small drop of rain in a ray of light. A break in the dam started as a small leak. A champion muscular weight lifter was once a baby that couldn't hold up his head. Your doctor was once in the first grade and didn't know how to spell his name. The first air flight was only a few hundred feet. A millionaire started with one dollar. Job 8:7 says; "Though thy beginning was small, yet thy latter end should greatly increase." Ecclesiastes 3:11 adds; "He hath made every thing beautiful in His time."

There is a cute story about an old clock that suddenly quit running. The reason the clock quit was because it had counted the number of times it would have to tick in one year; 31,538,000 times. This was far too many ticks for the tired and weary clock; so it lost its morale, its desire, and stopped ticking. Later it was explained to the clock that all that was expected of it was to tick just one tick at a time. With this understanding, it regained its spirit, its zeal and began ticking once more.

So it is with our married life. If we look at all the bumps in the road ahead or the path we have traveled over, we too may feel like just quitting. But God only asks us to live one moment, one day at a time. He promised in Isaiah 40:31; "They that wait upon the Lord shall renew their strength; they shall mount up with wings as eagles; they shall run, and not be weary; and they shall walk, and not faint." "God speaks to us through His providential workings and through the influence of His Spirit upon the heart. In our circumstances and surroundings, in the changes daily taking place around us, we may find precious lessons if our hearts are but open to discern them. The psalmist, tracing the work of God's providence, says, 'The earth is full of the goodness of the Lord.' 'Whoso is wise, and will observe these things, even they shall understand the loving-kindness of the Lord.' Psalm 33:5; 107:43."[7]

One of my sisters-in-law, Patty, gave me a gift mug on my 44th birthday. On it read "FROG," which stood for; "Fully Rely On God." That is the key to any happy home! Learning to trust Him for any and everything.

If your home is not happy look at the cause in your own heart. Probably you will find that you need to develop more self-control and less irritation, more deliberation and less impulsiveness, more faith and less doubt. An unhappy home is largely an internal heart problem. For out of the heart are the issues of life.

All the seminars, books, and marriage counseling in the world can't keep every marriage from breaking down. And there's the rub: Although research shows that Christian marriages have fewer problems than non-Christian marriages, they can still have problems. Marital trouble may not happen as frequently in a Christian home, but they still can arise.

When a conflict arises, pray that God will help. Don't let the devil use you as one of his tools to get to the other. Never allow yourself to yell or scream at your spouse, this only gives the devil more lead way. This is what the devil wants you to do. Nagging and playing mind games will cause your spouse to have more resistance. Allow the Holy Spirit to apply the pressure if pressure is what is needed. Don't play a junior Holy Spirit. He knows the best and only time to urge and when to back off.

The simple respect of not pushing or fault finding with the other will greatly reduce conflict. In other words, lead; don't push. When asking for forgiveness, also ask that your slate be wiped clean too. Apologize for your mistakes. It has never killed anyone yet. The key is to walk with Jesus. If opposition comes from your spouse, remember Scripture says: "If it be possible,...live peaceably with all men (*and women*). Dearly beloved, avenge not yourselves, but rather give place unto wrath: for it is written, Vengeance is mine; I will repay, saith the Lord." Romans 12:18, 19. (*Emphasis added*)

"Marriage, a union for life, is a symbol of the union between Christ and His church. The spirit that Christ manifests toward the church is the spirit that husband and wife are to manifest toward each other."[8]

Chapter 15

Making a loving and forgiving covenant between husband, wife, and children is a very important part of any marriage and family. If we are not faithful to each other 24 hours around the clock, then the family connection will suffer. Hearts will break, and children will often rebel against their parents. There must be found in every home, open communication, an atmosphere of freely offered grace to forgive each other with no holds bared. This and this alone are what will build a strong family unit.

Communication between all family members plays a huge part in families being able to work together as a whole unit. If the communication breaks down, then the family can never fully function as a total unit. It is very important to open up and leave channels open for each and every family member. This will keep the family running smoothly. God keeps His channels of communication open to us since we are a part of His family. He allows us freedom to speak and to tell Him what is on our hearts (see Palms 13). As a family unit, the channels must be allowed to stay open and things talked about that may be worrying one member or the other.

To conclude this chapter try to remember that it's during the storms of marriage or life itself that we come to know the great "I Am" and know what He can do. Try repeating the last words of the poem "Footprints" as your words. "My precious, precious child, I love you and I would never leave you. During your times of trail and suffering, when you see only one set of footprints, it was then that I carried you."

Reader, do you have problems in your marriage? Are there any storms brewing up between you and your spouse? Is there something going on in your marriage that you can't seem to handle? If there is, then take cheer because Jesus is on your side. Whatever you're facing, Jesus wants to be there with you. It doesn't matter what type of storm is hatching in your marriage. It could be financial or adultery. It might be personal or involve the whole family. Whatever you are facing, God is on your side. He repeats the same words to us today as He spoke to His disciples that night on the lake; "Be of good cheer. It is I. Do not be afraid."

Matthew 14:27. Jesus knows what you're going through. He knows that at times it's hard to see Him through the storm. He knows what we feel when our high expectation of Him seems to be unmeet.

"It is a solemn thing to die, but a far more solemn thing to live. Every thought and word and deed of our lives will meet us again. What we make of ourselves in probationary time, that we must remain to all eternity. Death brings dissolution to the body, but makes no change in the character. The coming of Christ does not change our characters; it only fixes them forever beyond all change."[9]

Chapter 16

"How to Survive and Revive a Dead Marriage"

In September of 1983, I held my very first crusade. Being one of those evangelists that likes catchy titles I had a sermon entitled; "Is There Sex After Death?" Any Bible searching Christian knows what the Bible teaches about death. "The dead know not anything." Ecclesiastes 9:5. When a person is laid to rest six feet under, "Their love, and their hatred, and their envy, is now perished....Whatsoever thy hand findeth to do, do it with thy might; for there is no work, nor device, nor knowledge, nor wisdom, in the grave, whither thou goest." Ecclesiastes 9:6, 10. Of course I hope you realize the sermon was on the state of the dead not sex. I ended the sermon with the text above and added, "If this verse is true, then I'm sorry to disappoint you but no, there is no sex after death." Many left that night with a sad look on their face. I guess they were hoping the Bible would tell them they were going to have a better sex life after they died than they were at that moment.

What about a marriage? Can it die also? And if so, what happens after the death of that marriage? Is it possible for a couple to be happy and survive while married in today's society? And why is it that the disease that brings on death in many marriages seems to attack shortly after leaving the altar with its cancer like cells eating away at the very core of what made you attracted to each other in the beginning? Since 1960 the United States has witnessed a quadrupling in the divorce rate. Marriages are dying faster than many want to admit. Neither this chapter nor book is written with all the answers to these and other questions you might have about surviving a dead marriage simply because every marriage is different and unique just like every individual is different and unique. But I do pray to give you hope if you are living in a dead marriage. Hope that might even save your marriage and prayerfully restore it back to life. For you see just as there is the assurance of a resurrection after death (see John 3:16) for those that trust and love Jesus, there is also the promise of a dead marriage being resurrected and restored to life. The same power and glory that will bring the dead back to life at the Second Coming can and will revive life to a vanished marriage today. "The grace of Christ, and this alone, can make this institution what God designed it should be—an agent for the blessing and uplifting of humanity. And thus the families of earth, in their unity and peace and love, may represent the family of heaven."[1]

I don't know why it is, but it seems that many of my marriage counseling consultations start off with the same excerpt. She says; "Our marriage started dying from the very beginning. After we were married, he stopped opening the door for me. He leaves his clothes all over the house. He never lowers the commode lid. He wants sex all the time." The men often start off asserting; "She leaves her hair on the floor and stockings hanging over the tub. She needs to take cooking lessons from my mother. She always has a headache when I approach her for sex, and she never dresses up sexy for me." Does any of this sound familiar? Need I say more? Most likely you're already well acquainted with those expressions and many more. "Our home here on earth is the place in which to prepare for the home above. If there are such temperaments in the family that they cannot live in harmony here, they would not, unless converted, be in harmony in the heavenly family."[2]

I've discovered during pastoral counseling most Christians seem to think they were to enjoy a happy marriage forever. They would never have any real problems. "After all," they will say, "Didn't God bring us together? Did He not join us together for life?" Just like a human's body begins to die the moment they are born, many marriages begin dying the moment a couple is joined together.

Chapter 16

For some, well, maybe I should say many, perhaps most, OK, the truth is all marriages have at one time or another become a battle ground for World War III. Sometimes this battle rages on for a duration of time, other times, just a short period. When you got married, you assumed your marriage was the perfect match. But soon you noticed landmines placed throughout the house waiting for someone, anyone to step on. It wasn't long until you found yourself walking on eggshells whenever your spouse was in a certain mood. At that time you began to wonder if instead of the perfect match that maybe your marriage was the perfect mismatch.

Why is it that many if not most marriages seem to have the perfect courtship while dating, but when the knot is tied, the rope starts to ravel shortly thereafter? I have mediated on that question time and time again. Then one day while studying I believe I came across the answer. The key to the answer is found in *Testimonies for the Church,* volume 7, and page 45. "Your education in married life has begun. *The first year of married life is a year of experience, a year in which husband and wife learn each other's different traits of character,* as a child learns lessons in school. In this, the first year of your married life, let there be no chapters that will mar your future happiness." (*Italics supplied*)

Could that be the answer? If we would just spend the first year of our married life *"learning,"* not *"changing," "each other's different traits of character."* If we did this then maybe we would understand better why our spouse does the things they do. But we are also told that "Satan is planning to take advantage of *our* hereditary and cultivated traits of character, and to blind *our eyes* to *our own* necessities and defects. Only through realizing our *own weakness* and looking steadfastly unto Jesus can we walk securely."[3]

Boy, how I wish I understood that twenty years ago when Kathy and I first got married. How much easier our married life would have been. Just think of the problems and misunderstandings we could have avoided if we had only realized how Satan would take advantage of our weaknesses and use them against us. He had us spend most of our time looking at each other's weaknesses instead of our own. And because we did not like what we saw, we spent the rest of the time trying to change the other to be like ourselves. When I think of all of those years we could have had happiness instead of sadness if we had only followed the counsel to *learn* each other's temperament instead of trying to *change* each other's natural temperament.

I think I know what some of you are thinking right now. "That would have been great if I had realized that too, but what do I do today, some numerous years later, with a dead or dying marriage?" Friend, that is a good question. How can we bring true happiness into our home today if we did not heed the counsel given to us so long ago? Well, guess what? I believe I found the answer to that question too. *"Make Christ first and last and best in everything*. Constantly behold Him, and your love for Him will daily become deeper and stronger as it is submitted to the test of trial. And *as your love for Him increases, your love for each other will grow deeper and stronger.* 'We all, with open face beholding as in a glass the glory of the Lord, are changed into the same image from glory to glory. 2 Corinthians 3:18.'"[4]

I believe that is the answer pure and sweet. By beholding Christ and lifting Him up, we can "survive" and "revive" any dying or dead marriage. It doesn't matter if you have been married less than a year or more than fifty, if you will pattern your life after Jesus', then your marriage will come back to life. How? Because your spouse will see Christ in you. *Ministry of Healing* page 360 adds; "As life with its burden of perplexity and care meets the newly wedded pair, the romance with which imagination so often invests marriage disappears. *Husband and wife learn each other's character as it was impossible to learn it in their previous association.* This is a most critical period in their experience. *The happiness and usefulness of their whole future life depend upon their taking a right course now. Often they discern in each other unsuspected weaknesses and defects;* but the hearts that love has united will discern excellencies also heretofore unknown. *Let all seek to discover the excellencies rather than the defects. Often it is our own attitude, the atmosphere that surrounds ourselves, which determines what will be revealed to us in another."* (*Italics supplied*)

Did you catch that last sentence? *"Often it is our own attitude, the atmosphere that surrounds ourselves"* that will determine how we will perceive our spouse. Wow! That means a happy marriage can be aroused from a dead marriage! All we have to do is change *our attitude* to be more like Christ and quit judging our spouse's weak points of character and start looking at their good points. If we will make it a point not to look at our spouse's imperfections, we will soon witness a change in their personality because they have seen a change in us. We will each enjoy watching the other receive victory through the transforming power of the Holy Spirit. This usually takes time, because our spouses like ourselves, have had years of bad habit experiences behind them that can only be overcome through the might and power of God's Spirit. We probably won't even notice the change at first, but the day will come when it will dawn on us that our spouse and we ourselves have become "new creatures." Claim this promise everyday: "The Lord has done great things for us, and we are glad." Psalms 126:3.

The Bible is clear that we should deal with others as we would want to be dealt with. "So in everything, do to others what you would have them do to you, for this sums up the Law and the Prophets." Matthew 7:12 NIV. The Golden Rule is truly golden. Our attitude toward one another can make all the difference in the world. Your spouse may just surprise you if given the opportunity. Your attitude toward your spouse can make a huge difference in surviving or reviving a dead marriage.

Years ago I watched a video titled "Johnny Lingo." The story was about an islander named Johnny Lingo who let the news out that he was out to find himself a wife. Now every father on the island wanted Johnny as a son-in-law because he was rich, strong, and very handsome.

A Powerful Marriage

As time continued every father brought his brightest, prettiest, and most intelligent daughter for Johnny to look over. Each father just knew they had the most beautiful daughter on the island, and Johnny for sure would pick his. But for some unknown reason to everyone's amazement, Johnny didn't choose any of the young beautiful women brought to him. Instead he chose for his bride the ugliest, most unwanted maiden on the whole island. Her father wouldn't even bring the young woman out to meet Johnny; he had to go to her.

After the news was out that Johnny had made his decision, he traveled over to meet the young maiden's father and offered him seven cows for her hand. This was more than any father on the island had ever been offered for his daughter. The entire island was shocked by Johnny's generosity. The father of the young maiden almost passed out. Soon after accepting Johnny's gallant proposal, the wedding of the century took place.

Later as the story progressed, the local storekeeper came upon Johnny and his new bride one bright and cheerful day. When Johnny's new wife came out from behind the shadow of the doorway, the storekeeper couldn't believe his eyes. This once ugly, unwanted maiden, was now beautiful. She was the most exquisite woman he had ever seen before. He couldn't help but ask Johnny what made the difference. Johnny said that after he paid more for her than any woman had ever been paid for before, she felt like a seven-cow woman. He made her feel beautiful, and she became beautiful.

This reminds me of the Bible story when Jacob worked for Laban to have the hand of Rachel in Genesis 29. "In early times custom required the bridegroom, before the ratification of a marriage engagement, to pay a sum of money or its equivalent in other property, according to his circumstances, to the father of his wife. This was regarded as a safeguard to the marriage relation. Fathers did not think it safe to trust the happiness of their daughters to men who had not made provision for the support of a family. If they had not sufficient thrift and energy to manage business and acquire cattle or lands, it was feared that their life would prove worthless. But provision was made to test those who had nothing to pay for a wife. They were permitted to labor for the father whose daughter they loved, the length of time being regulated by the value of the dowry required. When the suitor was faithful in his services, and proved in other respects worthy, he obtained the daughter as his wife; and generally the dowry which the father had received was given her at her marriage."[5]

What's the point? Simple. If you regard your spouse the way you would want to be regarded. If you hold dear and cherish them with unconditional love and let them know they are important to you, then chances are they will love, regard, value and cherish you in return. If they perceive they are free and at liberty to be themselves, allowed to experience life and to express their true character, then the breath of life will return to any dead marriage. Many will feel like a puppy that hasn't seen their master all-day—happy, content, satisfied, free, and blessed.

But if your spouse feels enclosed, trapped, smothered, or unloved, they might act like a caged beast wanting out. It is so easy to see the weakness of another person's character more than to see our own. "Neither the husband nor the wife should attempt to exercise over the other an arbitrary control. Do not try to compel each other to yield to your wishes. You cannot do this and retain each other's love. Be kind, patient, and forbearing, considerate, and courteous. By the grace of God you can succeed in making each other happy, as in your marriage vow you promised to do."[6]

Here's another example. Lets say you purchased a plastic teacup for $1.00 at the local "All's a Dollar" store. You know that a plastic teacup is strong and practically indestructible. So you feel free to take it on long trips across the country, camping trips and places that if it got misplaced or broken, you wouldn't lose sleep over it.

But now suppose you had another teacup made out of very breakable china costing one hundred and twenty-five dollars? It would not be the same old story would it? If it got broken or lost you probably would lose sleep, wouldn't you? In our home, Kathy and I have a beautiful Russian tea set we purchased on our first trip to Vologda, Russia. This delicate and fragile tea set came with a teapot and eight teacups. Each piece is painted with real gold around their rim and has a mother of pearl coating. Needless to say, we cherish them greatly. They were probably the most precious and cherished item we purchased in Russia.

Before our long trip home, we spared no expense on making sure that each piece was packed just right so they wouldn't break. We purchased a small wicker basket that looked like a picnic basket. We packed newspaper, towels, clothes, you name it, if it was soft, we wrapped it around this tea set. We didn't want to take any chance of the basket being tossed around like the airlines had already done too much of our luggage so we hand carried it on with us.

We made it home safely with our pride and joy without a scratch. They now sit in our china hutch for visitors to enjoy with us. This set in Russia had only cost thirty-five USA dollars. In Russia at that time it was worth one month's wage. I would have never been able to afford this set in America. To this day, whenever we show the set, we handle each piece with much care. And because we sanguines are known for dropping things, I let Kathy do most of the showing. I do not want to take a chance of scratching or dropping one cup.

This illustration demonstrates how various people value different things. If we give our spouse, or children for that matter, the insinuation that we don't think they are worth much, like maybe a $1.00 plastic teacup, then that is the way they will feel about themselves. But if we treat them like they are worth a million dollars or seven cows to us, then they will feel good about themselves and will most likely value you like you value them. Unfortunately, but some people find showing worth to others very difficult. For example, the choleric temperament finds it very difficult expressing pity. They perceive showing kindness and compassion as a sign of weakness and a waste of time. I have a good Christian friend with a strong choleric temperament that told me that he couldn't feel the hurt or heartache of his spouse. He also finds it very difficult to tell anyone they did a good job because he feels he could have done better. When he sees his melancholy wife hurting emotionally he becomes annoyed, impassive, and apathetic toward her. He has to make himself ask what is wrong. His first inclination is to tell her to pull herself together and get a life. But because of his born-again experience he finds himself being more sympathetic and compassionate to her even though he doesn't comprehend her grief.

Early in my ministry I discovered that many marriages were built on shifting sand. They never had any real foundation to stand on. Then one morning they woke up and found their marriage dead. We could compare this to "crib death." The night before all seemed to be OK. Then the next morning all life is gone. I have witnessed this sort of "crib death" with many marriages. They lose sight of their love for each other. And many times not only has the breath of life stopped in their relationship with each other, but also in their relationship with God. Spending time with each other everyday is very important. A good time for this is at mealtime. Ask each other how was their day and listen to their answer. But it is even more important to spend time eating Spiritual Bread with each other every day. Spending time in God's Word together is the breath to any marriage and is very essential to having a happy home. Pray that the Holy Spirit will guide each moment as you search for the truth God has given concerning how to have a happier marriage. Jesus Himself said of the Holy Spirit, "When He, the Spirit of truth, has come, He will guide you into all truth." John 16:13.

Always keep your focus on Christ and not on some other marriage. Looking at another couple's marriage will always disappoint you. He is the Bridegroom of all marriages. "The grace of Christ, and this alone, can make this institution what God designed it should be—an agent for the blessing and uplifting of humanity. And thus the families of earth, in their unity and peace and love, may represent the family of heaven."[7]

A good place to start building a happy marriage is on your knees. Reading your Bible along with the Spirit of Prophecy helps build strong marriages. Search to see what each has to say about having a happy marriage. And don't forget that there are many good books written on this very subject at your local ABC bookstore. Read them, hopefully together as a couple. But if one will not, and some temperaments will not see the need to do so, then do it alone. Ask God to lead you daily into knowing His will.

Satan often attacks a couple as soon as they leave the altar. This is not said to frighten or discourage but to warn you to brace yourself with Scripture and prayer. If this habit has formed at the beginning of your marriage probably no death has occurred. If not, at least form the habit now and you can survive any marriage. Whether your marriage is dead or alive, "Men and women may reach God's ideal for them if they will take Christ as their Helper."[8]

Chapter 17

"Strong to the Finish" [1]

"Many are seeking for happiness, but they know not how to obtain it. If such would find true happiness, their minds must first receive the right discipline. They must learn to have faith and confidence in God. Those who have not learned to subdue self, to control impulse, and to bring themselves into obedience to the principles of the law of God, will not, cannot be happy, or at peace and rest. They need the meekness and lowliness of Christ. They need to learn daily in his school, to wear his yoke, to lift his burdens, to deny inclination, to sacrifice a seeming present good for a future good, a personal advantage for a general advantage. The fountain of content must spring up in the soul. He who seeks happiness by changing his outward surroundings *without changing his own disposition*, will find that his efforts will produce only fresh disappointments. He carries himself with him wherever he goes. His unrest, his impatience, his uncontrollable thoughts and impulses, are ever present. The great trouble is in himself. Self has been cherished. He has never fallen upon the Rock and been broken. His will has never been trained to submit; his unyielding spirit has never been brought into subjection to the will of God."[2]

Have you ever thought of how a life, a ministry, a relationship, or a marriage ends up is very important to everything that goes before it! I believe it is.

Take for example Jim Baker or Jimmy Swaggart. Do you remember them? Now it's not a question on whether you liked them or not, it doesn't matter that thousands will tell you today that they were tremendously blessed and often encouraged by these men's ministries. Both of these men probably achieved many wonderful things during their ministry. Yet, today, what are their ministries remembered for? How they both ended, right?

Have any of you ever heard of the Buffalo Bills before? You probably have if you are a football fan like myself. Several years back they were the best team of the American Football League. For four years in a row, they traveled to the Super Bowl and lost every time. Each year they just knew this would be the season they would bring home the gold. But it never happened. So today to all of us football fans, we just smile and sometimes snicker whenever someone mentions the Buffalo Bills are in the playoffs and headed to the Super Bowl. And that's how they will be remembered for many years to come.

Think about Judas for a moment. Judas decided to follow Jesus one day. I'm sure he had heard Jesus preach many times. According to Matthew 10:1–8, all of the disciples went out healing the sick, casting out demons and preaching repentance. "And when he had called unto Him his twelve disciples, he gave them power against unclean spirits, to cast them out, and to heal all manner of sickness and all manner of disease…. These twelve Jesus sent forth, and commanded them, saying, Go not into the way of the Gentiles, and into any city of the Samaritans enter ye not: But go rather to the lost sheep of the house of Israel. And as ye go, preach, saying, The kingdom of heaven is at hand. Heal the sick, cleanse the lepers, raise the dead, cast out devils: freely ye have received, freely give."

Judas, along with the other eleven disciples, performed a lot of good deeds for the Kingdom of God. "He witnessed the Saviour's mighty works in healing the sick, casting out devils, and raising the dead…. He loved the Great Teacher, and desired to be with Him. He felt a desire to be changed in character and life, and he hoped to experience this through connecting himself with Jesus…. Jesus gave him a place among the twelve. He trusted him to do the work of an evangelist. He endowed him with power to heal the sick and to cast out devils."[3]

Chapter 17

Yet today how is Judas remembered? Basically only as the one that betrayed our Lord and Saviour.

Over the years of my ministry, I've watched good faithful members and even some men in the ministry make a huge mistake. Each loved and served their Saviour faithfully but in a split second, their life was ruined. All because they took their eyes off of Christ. And oftentimes when anyone mentions their names today, it's usually not the good they did for the Lord that is recalled, but how they ended their relationship with Christ and their marriage.

It's been some twenty years since I walked away from the drug scene I was in. Frequently whenever I run into one of my old drug buddies, all they want to talk about is our lives back when we partied and ran around having what we called fun. They do not recognize or understand the transformed man that stands before them now. They remember my life when we partied together. But my Christian friends today cannot imagine or fathom me with my past life. I'm thankful for this because I really don't want to be remembered that way.

Paul lived a long life. Many of those years he traveled the then known world telling others of Jesus. He lived and died serving his Saviour. But probably somewhere in the back of his mind he remembered the years when he worked against Christ's mission, when he had the orders in his hands to arrest the faithful followers of Jesus. Then the day came when he too was to be martyred for his faith in the Lord Jesus Christ. Listen to theses words Paul spoke in 2 Timothy 4:7,8 as he set in a Roman jail. As you read his words you can almost sense the incredible relief of his spirit as he writes: "I have fought a good fight, I have finished my course, I have kept the faith: Henceforth there is laid up for me a crown of righteousness, which the Lord, the righteous judge, shall give me at that day: and not to me only, but unto all them also that love his appearing."

How do you remember Paul today, his beginning or his end?

Yes my friend, how a life, a ministry, a relationship, or a marriage ends up is more important than everything that goes before it! Only Jesus knows our past and what the future holds in store because of the results of our past. "He (Jesus) alone is acquainted with the past life of the person, and what his future will be."[4]

The Bible tells us in Hebrews 12:1-3; "Wherefore seeing we also are compassed about with so great a cloud of witnesses, let us lay aside every weight, and the sin which doth so easily beset us, and let us run with patience the race that is set before us, Looking unto Jesus the author and finisher of our faith; who for the joy that was set before him endured the cross, despising the shame, and is set down at the right hand of the throne of God. For consider him that endured such contradiction of sinners against himself, lest ye be wearied and faint in your minds."

I would like to end this book by talking to you about finishing the race you started in your marriage. Perhaps it's a race you entered some time ago or possibly just recently started running. Whichever your case may be, chances are when you voiced the words "I do" you left the starting line running with a full burst of speed. Happy, excited, electrified and thrilled knowing you married the perfect mate. With ease you jumped each hurdle that stood in your way. But as the race continued you soon realized that the barriers you were jumping got higher with each leap. The pain of not being understood grew each day and dark clouds started shadowing the racetrack. You fell a time or two but always got back up. But the strife and confusion of married life came like a sudden downpour of rain and the wind blew stronger. Soon came a hailstorm that destroyed whatever was left of the race. Your wounds became contaminated and infected and thoughts of quitting the race crossed your mind.

Let me re-read Hebrews 12:1 from the NIV to you. "Therefore, since we are surrounded by such a great cloud of witnesses, let us throw off everything that hinders and the sin that so easily entangles, and let us run with perseverance the race marked out for us."

Chapter 17

That "P" word "perseverance," King James calls it "patience"; the New King James says "endurance," we don't like much! It means we will have to work at what we are to do. The verse simply says: "Let us run with perseverance the race *marked* out for us." And verse two adds while running: "We must keep our *eyes fixed* on Jesus."

As a teenager in Boy Scouts we often would have something like a cross-country relay race where we would have to run against other scout troops. I remember the time I started off one of these races with a bang. Along the path different Scoutmasters were placed to point us in the right direction, which trails to take and when to turn. Sometimes we would have to stop and do a certain amount of push-ups, sit-ups, or chin-ups. I knew that if I ever intended to win a ribbon I would have to do exactly what they said to do. I couldn't say to myself. "Let's see. The Scoutmaster back there told me to run this way for one mile before I turn. But I know that if I turn here and run over this hill, I could cut that mile in half. I'm sure he would not mind." No it didn't work that way. I had to run with determination and perseverance the trail that had been marked out for me to run.

And so it is with the race of marriage. Each of us must run the trail and course that God has set before us. I realize and understand that these courses are not always easy to run. But always keep in retrospect that God has gone before us. He knows the obstacles that get in our way that may cause us to take a detour. He understands the pain and hurt that comes with many marriages. He hears us when we cry out that not all is okay on the racetrack. Just like there were Scoutmasters along the course telling me which way to go and when to turn, God has placed His holy angles along the course we run in our marriage to tell us which way to turn and what path to take. That is why He can say to us that we should "Run the race of marriage with perseverance and determination." You and I must be determined and have it settled in our own mind that we are going to make our marriage work no matter what it takes. Until this is done, then our running will be in vain.

A Powerful Marriage

Always keep in mind that every marriage is unique and different. Just like no two people have the exact temperament blend, every marriage has its different path or trail to run. Something I've discovered while conducting marriage counseling is that many married couples like to compare their marriage with another couple's marriage. And this is a huge no-no!

When a marriage gets rough and tough it is easy to start feeling sorry for oneself. And if we are not careful we may find ourselves thinking things like; "If only my marriage was like Bob's and Janet's. They were made for each other." "If only my wife understood me like Betty understands Joe, then we wouldn't have the problems we do." "I could handle the problems that Jerry and Marlene have in their marriage. At least he allows her to speak her feelings." "If I had her husband I could run with all sorts of perseverance and determination." Or we might simply say, "My marriage is so much harder to run than anyone else's. Lord, I'm quitting this race because I just don't have enough perseverance."

I could write more but I believe you get the picture. We can rationalize ourselves to the point that we finally give up and quit running our race altogether. But God says, "I want you to run the race that is yours to run. I don't want you to think about another's marriage, just keep your eyes focused on Me. If you do that then we will run this race together. And remember if you plan to finish the race, you have to keep running until you reach the finish line."

I heard a sermon once using the following example about a man running in a race. This man had what it took to finish. Talk about perseverance and determination!

It was around 7:00 PM October 20, 1968. The sun was going down, and it was starting to cool down and get dark at the Mexico City Olympics Stadium. The last of the Olympic Marathon Runners were being assisted away to different first-aid stations and soon the last few thousand spectators began to leave. When all of a sudden a blast of police sirens and whistles were heard. The focus of every eye was toward the gate at the entrance of the stadium.

Chapter 17

With everyone's attention turned to the gate, in limped a sole runner wearing the colors of Tanzania. He was the last runner to finish the Marathon Race in 1968. His leg was bandaged and bloody because earlier in the race he had taken a bad fall, and now it was all he could do to limp his way across the track.

The crowed stood and applauded him as he completed his last lap around the track. When he finally crossed the finish line, someone asked him the question that everyone was wondering. "Since you are so badly injured, why didn't you quit? Why didn't you just give up?" And John Steven Aquari's answer was; "My country did not send me seven thousand miles to start this race. My country sent me to finish this race."

And friend, so it is with the race that God gave us to run. He didn't ask us to just start running. He asked us to finish! God has asked us all to both start and finish every race we begin.

Do you remember any marathon races you may have competed in while still in school? You probably were full of energy at first. You felt strong and ready to tackle anything that got in your way. For months you exercised and trained just for the moment when the gun would go off. Excitement ran through your veins until the moment finally arrived.

I would like to forget the time our church wanted to have a Fun Run to raise funds for a project we had going. Several years before this event took place I had lost some weight and had taken up jogging. I finally got where I could jog quite a distance before tiring out. Well, over the course of time, I had gained a few of those pounds back and had not laced up my jogging shoes for months. But I felt I could still jog without too much of a problem. This was going to be the day I had trained for years before. I was sure I wouldn't win because I knew the other men and women I would be running against. But who cared? I just wanted to finish.

When the gun sounded, I was off like a flash of lighting. I did pretty well for the first, oh two minutes or so. We had not even rounded the first corner yet when I started tiring out fast. I was determined to finish no matter what because passing me were women, children and older folks. I was not to be done in by a seven and seventy-seven year old!

Well, to make a long story short, I did finish but not until I had blisters on both of my feet. My legs felt like oatmeal and my muscles were screaming. Oh yes, I walked more than half of it. In fact almost all of it. And from that moment on my whole outlook on marathon running changed forever. The truth is, I wanted to quit after the first few minutes of running. But I had been bragging that "this race was going to be easy. A piece of cake. Anyone could do it."

Today I feel that marriage is like a marathon race. We start off our marriage running with a huge bang. But after we travel down the rocky road a bit, we find out that often pain is involved with the running. That it is going to take a lot more perseverance and determination than what we ever dreamed we would need. More persistence and firmness of mind than what we imagined was possible.

Almost any married couple will tell you that even with perseverance and determination, pain and hurt is involved in making a marriage work. So much pain that you wonder if God is even with you during the difficult times of your marriage. But friends, if you have not learned anything else from this book, learn this. Just because pain is sometimes involved with making a marriage race work, doesn't mean God is not there running the race with you.

No matter what particular race you are running at this moment, run it with all you got. And if you should slip, fall and make a mistake, or should your spouse make a mistake (again), then get up and continue running.

Have you ever heard of the movie "Chariots of Fire?" It was a true story about a man named Eric Liddell. Eric was from Scotland and ran in the Olympics of 1924. He was to run in the 440. Shortly after the gun sounded Eric had only run but a few feet when his feet got tangled up with another runner's and fell.

Chapter 17

As he sat there dazed and not knowing what to do, an official screamed at him to "Get up and run." He leaped to his feet and started running again. By this time he could tell that the other runners were a good twenty yards ahead of him. Somehow he mustered more speed and ran with all he had. Soon he found himself 4th place. Then 3rd. In no time he was in 2nd place. There was only one more runner in front of him. And just as they crossed over the finish line, Eric stuck out his chest and won the race. He collapsed in total exhaustion and had to be helped off the track, but he had won! The newspaper the next morning reported that "His win was the greatest track performance they had ever seen."

Over the years I have come to realize something very important. There's something always glorious about getting up after you have been knocked down. Because win or lose, you didn't stay down. Some of you reading this book have been knocked down and tripped up by Satan time and time again. He's caused you to make some bad decision in your marriage and everyday living. At times you feel ashamed, embarrassed, depressed, or self-pity. And at moments like this you want to do nothing better than to stay down on the track and hope that no one notices you as they run by. But Gods has a message for all of us when we feel this way. He says "Get up and run!

Philippians 1:6 does not say: "He who began a good work in you will carry it on to completion until the day you fail and flop on the track." No! But what it does say is: "He who began a good work in you will carry it on to completion until the day of Jesus Christ."

You remember the story when Jesus was talking to Peter in Matthew 26:34 and again in John 21:15–19. Jesus was saying: "Peter the time is quickly coming when you are going to deny me. And after you do, I want you to get back up and finish the race. Don't stay down, but get up and run. And keep running no matter what the cost." You know I believe that is still good advice for us today.

In the marathon race in Boston you will find a legendary obstacle called "Heartbreak Hill." It is the longest, hardest, and steepest hill of the whole race. It will put the strongest runner to the test. It will separate the men from the boys. And only the best of the best make it over this monster of a hill.

Often marriages must go over "Heartbreak Hills." No one ever said that marriage would always be run on a level plain. There will always be ups and downs. You will find walls often placed right before you. There will be times when you seem to have come to the end of your rope.

Years back while living in Iowa, one of my dear members who was ninety-five years old at that time gave me a quote I've kept for years. I've used it over and over in my life. Whether it is in my marriage or some other race it has helped me many times. Bernice Taylor said; "When you reach the end of your rope—tie a knot and hang on."

Friend, when you feel you have reached the end of your rope, your "Heartbreak Hill," then tie a knot and hang on. James 1:12 says, "Blessed is the man that endureth temptation: for when he is tried, he shall receive the crown of life, which the Lord hath promised to them that love him." The knot to hang onto is Jesus. He is our rope, our strength.

Soon we are all going home. This old world is almost over. That is why we must keep placing one foot in front of the other in all of our races. Hebrews 12:2 says: "Looking unto Jesus, the Author & Finisher of our faith." He is the one and only one that can see us to the finish line.

There is another race that is often run. It is the race where a baton or torch is held and passed on to the next runner. And they keep on passing the torch or baton until the race is finished.

Even though marriage life has its "Heartbreak Hills," and the devil trips us up, with each passing day we get that much closer to the finish. Someday we all will be able to stick out our chest as we cross over the finish line and win this race. Then we can hand Jesus our torch and thank Him for keeping it burning for us. And then we can repeat the final words of the Apostle Paul: "We have fought the good fight. We have finished the race. We have kept the faith."

But until that day, we must keep running.

"Let the home be full of sunshine. This will be worth far more to your children than lands or money. Let the home love be kept alive in their hearts that they may look back upon the home of their childhood as a place of peace and happiness next to heaven."[5]

Upon The Cross

Upon the cross He spread His wings,
And gave to life a Saviour's death.
He proclaimed heaven's victory
    With His final breath.

Upon the cross He gave a gift,
The gift of everlasting life.
A promise that someday we'll live,
In a world without it's strife.

Upon the cross He gave His Word,
A promise with majestic voice.
"I'll die this day, but will return,"
A death for life was His choice.

Upon the cross He became our sin,
So that all could achieve.
A wisdom of His divine love,
A gift to those who believe.

—by David A. Farmer, Jr.

INDEX TO REFERENCES
Introduction

1. *Patriarchs and Prophets, p. 175*
2. *ibid. p. 189*
3. *Gospel Workers, p. 125 (Italics supplied) (IS)*
4. *Ministry of Healing p. 359 (IS)*
5. *Solemn Appeal, 1870 p. 104*
6. *Testimonies for the Church, vol. 5, p. 42*
7. *Signs of the Times, 1886 (IS)*
8. *Testimonies for the Church, vol. 4, p. 504 (IS)*
9. *Thoughts from Mount of Blessings, p. 63*
10. *Testimonies for the Church, vol. 5, p. 362 (IS)*
11. *Testimonies for the Church vol. 7, p. 45*
12. *Testimonies for the Church vol. 3, p. 325*
13. *Review and Herald, 1892 (IS)*

Chapter 1
"Learning to Live Happily Ever After"

1. *Honey I Love You, But Why Are We So Different? p. 66 (IS)*
2. *Solemn Appeal, p. 120 (IS)*
3. *The Ministry of Healing, p. 362 (IS)*
4. *Grand Rapids, Mich.: Fleming H. Revell, 1967, pp. 160-161*
5. *Patriarchs and Prophets, 426 (IS)*
6. *Notebook Leaflets, p. 74*
7. *Testimonies for the Church, vol. 7, p. 45 (IS)*
8. *Testimonies for the Church, vol. 8, p. 314 (IS)*
9. *Gospel Workers, p. 473 (IS)*

Chapter 2
"What are Temperaments?"

1. *Anon. The Ministry of Healing, p. 361, 362*
2. *Testimonies for the Church, vol. 4, p. 69*

Chapter 3
"University of Hard Knocks"

1. *Ministry, January 1997, p. 18*
2. *Signs of the Times, 1897*
3. *Review and Herald, 1882*
4. *Testimonies for the Church, vol. 3, p. 504 (IS)*
5. *Testimonies for the Church, vol. 8, p. 314*

Chapter 4
"Lord Have Mercy. I Married a Motor-Mouth Joker: The Sanguine"

1. Testimony to Ministers and Workers, No. 9, 1898
2. Steps to Christ, p. 63

Chapter 5
"Help! I Married an Egotistical and Domineering Workaholic: The Choleric"

1. Counsels in Parents, Teachers, Students, p. 94
2. Review and Herald, 1886 (IS)

Chapter 6
"The Six Million Dollar Man and the Bionic Woman: The Melancholy"

1. Ministry of Healing, p. 480
2. Patriarchs and Prophets, p. 176 (IS)
3. Ministry of Healing, p. 247

Chapter 8
"There is Hope"

1. Bible Echo, 1899
2. See SDA Commentary, vol. 3, p. 926
3. Thoughts From the Mount of Blessing, p. 65, 66
4. Ministry of Healing, p. 249 (IS)
5. Ibid., p. 249 (IS)
6. Signs of the Times, 1886 (IS)
7. Steps to Christ, p. 117
8. Signs of the Times, 1890
9. See Testimonies for the Church, vol. 2, p. 306
10. The Great Controversy, p. 508

Chapter 9
"Determinations"

1. Christ's Object Lesson, p. 250
2. Signs of the Times, 1902
3. The Ministry of Healing, p. 360 (IS)
4. Testimonies for the Church, vol. 3, p. 323

Chapter 10
"Mask or Not to Mask; That is the Question"

1. *Christ's Object Lesson, p. 331 (IS)*
2. *Maranatha, p. 237*
3. *Review and Herald, 1890 (Emphasis added)*
4. *Maranatha, 237*
5. *Review and Herald, 1886*
6. *Ministry of Healing, p. 256*
7. *Testimonies for the Church, vol. 8, p. 172*
8. *The Desire of Ages, p. 232*
9. *Review and Herald, 1892*

Chapter 11
"Myths of a Happy or Miserable Marriage"

1. *Examples, Pastor Rick Warren*
2. *Ministry of Healing, p. 356*
3. *Review and Herald, 1868*
4. *Review and Herald. 1886*
5. *Testimonies for the Church, vol. 2, p. 99*
6. *ibid, p. 418*
7. *SDA Commentary, vol. 6, p. 1093 (IS)*
8. *Ministry of Healing, p. 361*
9. *Pamphlets, 1892*
10. *Testimonies for the Church, vol. 7, p. 45 (IS)*
11. *Testimonies vol. 7, p. 45 (IS)*
12. *Signs of the Times, 1903-06*
13. *Early Writings, p. 295 (IS)*
14. *The Great Controversy, p. 598*

Chapter 12
"The Y2Khaos of Marriage."

1. *Patriarchs and Prophets, p. 46*
2. *Patriarchs and Prophets, p. 53*
3. *Patriarchs and Prophets, p. 46*
4. *Mount of Blessings, p. 63*
5. *Ministry, January 1997, p. 18*
6. *Multnomah Books, 1993*
7. *Testimonies for the Church, vol. 2, p. 417*
8. *Testimonies for the Church, vol. 7, p. 50 (IS)*
9. *Review and Herald, 1904*
10. *Bible Echo, 1899*
11. *General Conference Bulletins, 1903*
12. *Testimonies for the Church, vol. 2, pp. 355-356*

Chapter 13
"God's Pillars for a Happy Marriage"

1. Bible Echo, 1887
2. Review and Herald, 1886 (Emphasis added)
3. ibid.
4. Harper Collins Publishers, page 318
5. The Desire of Ages, p. 331
6. Patriarchs and Prophets, p. 69
7. Patriarchs and Prophets, p. 57, 58
8. Christian Education p. 237
9. Patriarchs and Prophets, p. 48
10. Patriarchs and Prophets. p. 32

Chapter 14
"Why Do Such Good Looking Ladies Marry Such Ugly Looking Men?"

1. The Ministry of Healing, p. 361 (IS)
2. In Testimonies for the Church, vol. 2, page 465
3. Patriarchs and Prophets, p. 44
4. Patriarchs and Prophets, p. 46
5. Patriarchs and Prophets, p. 338
6. Baker Books, 1991
7. Review and Herald, 1882
8. Education, p. 219
9. Review and Herald, 1886
10. Solemn Appeal, 1870 p. 176

Chapter 15
"The Storms of Marriage"

1. Examples, Pastor D. Z. Cofield
2. Christ's Object Lesson, p. 178
3. The Desire of Ages, p. 380 (Emphasis added)
4. Review and Herald, 1902
5. Vol. 5, p. 348
6. ibid., p. 356 (Emphasis added)
7. Steps to Christ, p. 87
8. Testimonies for the Church, vol. 7, p. 46
9. Testimonies for the Church, vol. 5, p. 466

Chapter 16
"How to Survive and Revive a Dead Marriage"

1. Thoughts From the Mount of Blessing, p. 65

2. *Review and Herald, 1886*
3. *The Desire of Ages, p. 382 (Emphasis added)*
4. *Testimonies for the Church, vol. 7, p. 46 (IS)*
5. *Patriarchs and Prophets, p. 188*
6. *The Ministry of Healing, p. 361*
7. *Thoughts From the Mount of Blessing, p. 65*
8. *Testimonies for the Church, vol. 7, p. 49*

Chapter 17
"Strong to the Finish"

1. *Examples, Pastor Craig Brian Larson*
2. *Review and Herald, 1886 (IS)*
3. *Desire of Ages, p. 716*
4. *Pamphlets, 97.059*
5. *Patriarchs and Prophets, p. 176*

We'd love to send you a free catalog of titles we publish
or even hear your thoughts, reactions, criticism,
about things you did or didn't like about this
or any other book we publish.

Just write or call us at:

TEACH Services, Inc.
1-800/367-1998

www.tsibooks.com